BUTTERICK'S

Fast & Easy
Needlecrafts

BUTTERICK'S
Fast & Easy Needlecrafts

Over 50 Fashion
and Decorating Projects
You Can Make
in Less Than a Day

Bella Scharf

Butterick Publishing

This book is dedicated to my parents.

Illustrations: Bella Scharf
Inking: Phoebe Gaughan
Photography: Bob Connolly
Book Design: Angela Foote
Cover Design: Winifred Young

Copyright © 1977 by
Butterick Publishing
161 Sixth Avenue
New York, N.Y. 10013

A Division of American Can

Library of Congress Catalog Card Number: 76-56596
International Standard Book Number: 0-88421-029-4

Manufactured in the United States of America

Contents

Best Projects for Beginners

Introduction

For a craft to become a worthwhile, enjoyable hobby, your initial experiences with it must be successful. The feeling of accomplishment you derive from completing your first few projects will motivate you to try more challenging ones. The sooner a project is successfully completed, the sooner you experience the gratification of having created something beautiful and useful. As a beginner, your ideal choice for a first project would be one involving basic techniques, requiring few tools and small amounts of materials. Crocheting a hat, making a macramed choker, or appliquéing a pot holder can be a perfect way to practice your newly learned skills in each of these three crafts; at the same time you are creating useful and decorative accessories.

Simple projects that can be completed quickly will appeal to the experienced needleworker as well. If you have already braved the challenge of crocheting an afghan, knotting an intricate macramed hanging, or making a bed-size quilt, you know that these projects can sometimes take months of patient labor to complete. There are hazards to undertaking major projects, as many craft enthusiasts have found. Often, you may buy all the necessary materials, begin the project, and then find that your schedule does not allow you sufficient time to devote to it. Your frustration causes you to lose interest in the project and, possibly, in the craft. Simple, attractively designed craft items that you can make quickly and inexpensively may be the answer for you.

This book offers a collection of projects that are easy to do and can be completed in a short period of time. Some items can be made in an hour, some in one evening, and some in three or four afternoons.

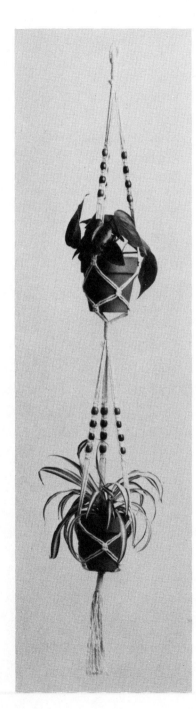

Though your expertise and speed in the craft will determine the amount of time and effort you invest, none of these projects requires more than two weeks of part-time work to complete.

Featured are over fifty projects with step-by-step instructions, and dozens of suggestions for putting these designs to other uses. The projects are done in the speediest and most popular needlecraft techniques: crochet, macrame, needlepoint, bargello, appliqué, patchwork, quilting, and embroidery. The fundamentals of each of these crafts appear in chapter 1, covering materials and tools, basic procedures, and finishing techniques. These basics are an elementary course in each craft and you should learn or review them before starting any project.

The emphasis in each project is not only on speed and simplicity, but also on esthetic appeal and function. Each design presented will inspire you by showing how easily you can incorporate the charm of a handcrafted look into your home and wardrobe. The projects are grouped by category, each grouping designed to fill basic home decorating and fashion accessorizing needs. One chapter features designs for belts, handbags, jewelry, hats, shawls, and even a simple way to trim store-bought clothes. In the chapter on small home accessories there is a collection of items ranging from pot holders, pillows, afghans, and lampshades, to a method for recycling empty wine bottles to transform them into flower vases. Various methods for displaying live plants and for decorating walls are presented in two other chapters, each design executed in a different craft technique. Any of these fashion and home accessories would be an ideal gift item, and chapter 6 offers even more

gift ideas to consider. Included is a paperback book cover, a picture frame, ideas for making personalized accessories, and even designs for greeting cards.

In making any of these projects you are assured that your completed piece will look very much like the one pictured if you use the same materials and colors. But you are also free, if you wish, to exercise your imagination and change the design to suit your own taste. You could make the item in your favorite colors, or in shades to match your home's decor, using the color plates only as suggestions for coloration. Each item can be made in any one of a variety of materials. The crocheted lampshade, for example, can be constructed from worsted yarn, as well as from such finer materials as crochet cotton or metallic yarn. Each material will achieve a different effect. In addition, many projects enable you to use up materials that you may have left over as scraps from other projects, so the expense in making many of these items is minimal.

Whether you are an experienced or a novice needleworker, you will be impressed by the visual presentation of each project, and will find it a remarkable aid. Each item's instructions are accompanied by explicit illustrations, showing how the item should be constructed from start to finish.

The attractive, useful projects in this book, with their easy-to-follow illustrated instructions, can be made quickly by practically anyone. Young and old, male and female, everyone can enjoy the many pleasures of handcrafts as a leisure-time activity.

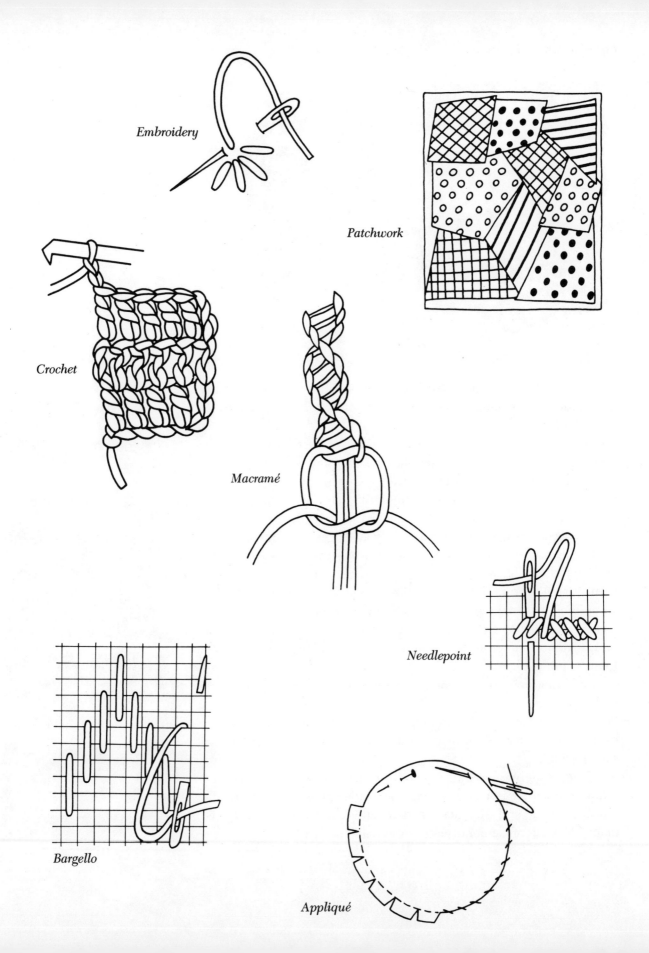

Embroidery

Patchwork

Crochet

Macramé

Needlepoint

Bargello

Appliqué

The Basics ══════════1

Needlepoint

NEEDLEPOINT IS THE craft of stitching with thread or yarn on open-weave stiff canvas, working the needle in and out of the holes of the weave. Unlike embroidery, where stitching is done only in one area of the fabric leaving the rest of the fabric plain, in needlepoint the entire canvas is filled with stitches.

Canvas

Needlepoint canvas can have as many as 18 holes to the inch (18-mesh) or as few as 5 holes to the inch (5-mesh). Naturally, stitching on canvas with fewer holes per inch is quicker and easier, so most of the needlepoint projects presented in this book are designed for 10-mesh and 5-mesh canvas. The size of the canvas describes the number of mesh (threads) per inch. For example, #10 canvas has 10 mesh to the inch. Also, these are the sizes most available in craft and department stores.

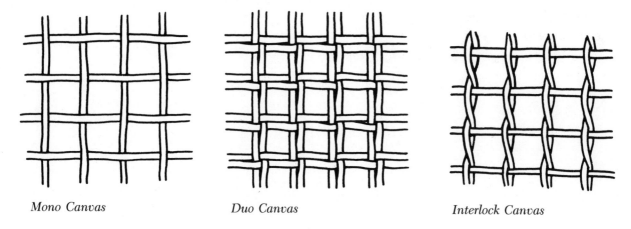

Mono Canvas   Duo Canvas   Interlock Canvas

Figure 1

Canvas is manufactured in three types of weaves: *mono canvas*, a simple weave; *duo canvas*, which is a simple weave but has two threads separating the holes rather than one; and *interlock canvas*, which has horizontal threads secured in place by twisted vertical threads (Figure 1). Bargello can be done on any of these canvases, but the half cross stitch and cross stitch should be done on either duo or interlock canvas.

Figure 2

Needles

The tapestry needle is made of metal, has a large eye to accomodate the thickness of the yarn, and has a blunt point (Figure 2). A 2″ long needle, Size 18 or 19, is suitable for working on 10-mesh canvas; a 2½″ long needle, Size 13, is best for working on 5-mesh canvas.

Yarns

Unlike knitting yarns, yarns for needlepoint are spun to have very little stretch. The best yarn to use for working on 10-mesh canvas is 3-strand Persian-type yarn, either wool or acrylic. It consists of three strands which can be separated and worked with individually, each strand made up of 2-ply threads twisted together. All three strands are threaded together into the needle for working the half cross stitch and cross stitch on 10-mesh canvas. For bargello, it may sometimes be necessary to fold the yarn in half and work with double strands. Wool or cotton tapestry yarn can also be used, as well as a less expensive and more available substitute—4-ply worsted yarn. For working on 5-mesh canvas you can use either one strand of rug yarn, or two or three strands of worsted or tapestry yarn used together as one.

The canvas must be covered completely with none of the weave showing through the stitching. Before starting any project it is essential to make a sample of the stitch pattern with the yarn you wish to use. For 10-mesh canvas you should experiment by working the pattern first with 1 strand and then with 2 strands of yarn to determine which combination would best cover the canvas. For 5-mesh canvas try two strands, three strands, or two doubled strands. The stitches should not be so tight as to pull apart the threads of the weave. In this way you could also determine whether to use scraps of yarn of other weights and textures, such as baby yarn, sport yarn, metallic yarn, rattail yarns, and others.

Estimating Amounts of Yarn to Use

An estimate of the amount of yarn required is given for each project. The exact quantity necessary to complete the item will depend on what kind of yarn you use and how tightly you work the stitches. It is a good idea to purchase more than you think will be required, to make sure you will have enough yarn in an exact matching color. (Dye lots vary. You can use the leftovers for smaller items.)

Since Persian yarn usually comes pre-cut into working lengths, you can work an area with one strand. Based on the amount of coverage this one strand achieves, you can estimate how many strands you will need to cover the entire area.

Binding the Edges of the Canvas

Any needlepoint piece should have a 1″ allowance of canvas all around the design area which will not be stitched. To prevent the cut edges of the canvas from fraying while the piece is being worked, glue masking tape onto the raw edges, with half the tape covering the front of the edge, the other half folded over to cover the back edge.

Beginning and Ending a Row

Thread the needle with a strand of yarn no longer than 24″. If the strand is longer, it will go through the holes of the canvas too many times, causing a great deal of abrasion, resulting in thinning and shredding of the yarn.

After threading the strand into the needle, do not knot the end. Instead, bring the needle through a hole to the right side, leaving a 1″ tail on the wrong side. Then stitch the first few stitches over the tail, securing it to the canvas (Figure 3).

Once the strand is too short to make any more stitches, bring the needle to the wrong side and weave it through the back of a few stitches. Clip the remainder of the strand.

Figure 3

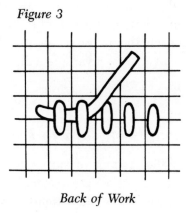

Back of Work

Blocking

Canvas is usually pulled out of shape by stitches, especially by the diagonal half cross stitch. To restore it to its original shape once the stitching is done, roll the stitched piece in a damp towel to moisten it. Then lay it face down on an ironing board or other board into which you can push pins. Form it to the desired shape and insert pins all around the edge to secure it in this shape. Let it dry. An easier method, though it tends to flatten the texture of the stitches, is to press the right side of the work. Place a wet paper towel or press-cloth on top of the stitching, then move a hot iron on top of it, barely touching the cloth.

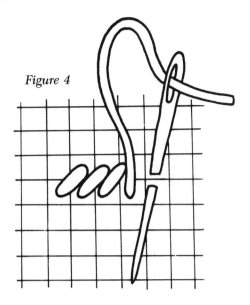

Figure 4

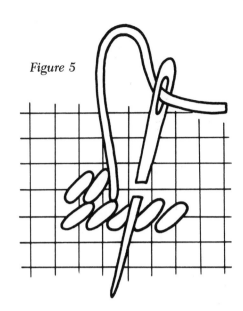

Figure 5

The Half Cross Stitch

The effect of many small diagonal stitches formed by the half cross stitch is considered to be the classic needlepoint stitch. This diagonal stitch is used for filling in intricate, detailed designs since it is small and can be stitched to follow the most sinuous outlines. There are three different methods of forming this stitch: the Continental or tentstitch, the basketweave stitch, and the half cross. The easiest of these is the half cross stitch.

Starting at the left, bring the needle up at A, go down into the canvas at B, then up again at C (Figure 4). It is not necessary to go down into the hole and come up again in the next hole in one motion. Sometimes this one-step stitching causes abrasion in the yarn by pulling it too rapidly through the stiff canvas. It is usually better to push the needle through the hole completely to the back, pulling the yarn with it, then bring the needle and yarn up through the next hole.

Once a row of half cross stitches is completed, turn the canvas around and work the second row across, again going from left to right the same way (Figure 5).

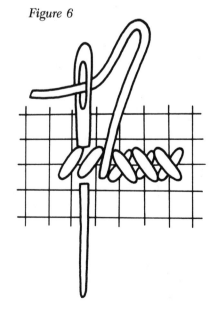

Figure 6

The Cross Stitch

Work a row of half cross stitches from left to right. Then, without turning the canvas around, make half cross stitches again from right to left, working into the same holes as the first row. The half cross stitches thus become cross stitches (Figure 6).

Bargello

Bargello, also called *Florentine stitch,* is the technique of covering canvas with long vertical stitches, usually in a symmetrical wave pattern which forms a decorative, fabric-like effect. Each stitch can cover as few as three threads or as many as six or seven threads of canvas at once. The technique is easy to master because once the pattern is established by the first row, you simply work each successive row to follow the same pattern.

Graphs for different bargello patterns are presented throughout the book. Since the technique of forming the zigzag pattern is always the same, learn and practice the following basic bargello *flame* pattern:

Figure 7

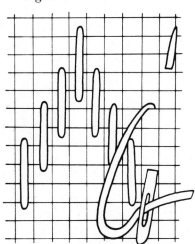

Figure 8

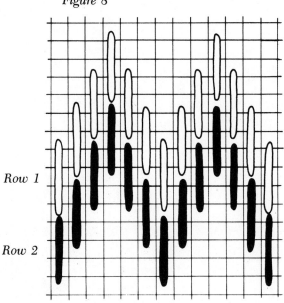

Row 1

Row 2

Figure 9

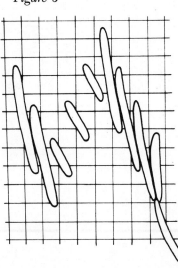

Figure 10

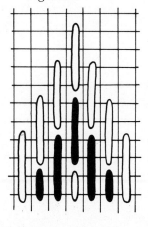

From left to right—Top row: Basic bargello pattern (chapter 1). Two repeats of diamond pattern of bargello belt (chapter 2). Middle row: Paperback book cover pattern (chapter 6). Diamond-shaped bargello pillow appliqué pattern (chapter 3). Bottom row: Bargello picture appliqué pattern (chapter 3). Variation of preceding pattern—work a few rows of pattern, then turn canvas around and work same pattern on the other side of starting row; fill in centers.

Come up at A, go down at B, covering four threads. Come up at C, go down at D. Follow Figures 7 and 8 to complete the first row, making a few more repeats of the pattern than are shown in Figure 8, for practice. Then work Row 2 in another color yarn below Row 1. As you can see, the top of the stitches of Row 2 share the same holes as the bottom of the stitches of Row 1. Figure 9 shows the back of the work—working up, long diagonal stitches are formed; working down, the stitches are short and diagonal. Once the canvas is filled with pattern rows, it is necessary to fill in the unworked areas of canvas on top and bottom, adjusting the length of the stitches to form a straight line on either edge (Figure 10).

The Chain Stitch

This stitch, similar to chain stitch in embroidery, can serve as a border around areas worked in other stitches.

Bring the needle up through one hole. Insert it again into the same hole and then up through the hole above it, picking up one thread of canvas. Place the yarn over the needle and pull the needle through (Figure 11). For the second, and all successive stitches, insert the needle into the same hole through which it was just pulled, then up through the hole above it. Form the stitch the same way as the first.

Figure 11

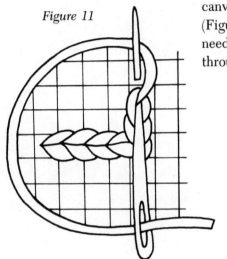

The Overcast Stitch

This stitch can serve as a border on the very edge of a stitched piece whose raw edges have been folded and basted to the back.

Thread the needle with a double strand of yarn so that the stitching will fully cover the edge. Then overcast all around the edge, working a stitch in every hole and over the fold of the canvas. Make three stitches into every corner (Figure 12).

Figure 12

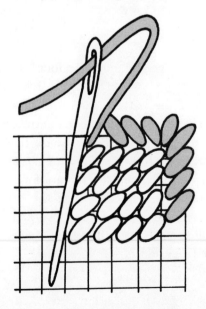

Embroidery

EMBROIDERY IS THE craft of stitching with yarn or thread on fabric, using a variety of stitches to form decorative designs. The stitching can cover the fabric completely, though it is usually worked only in one area with the unstitched fabric forming a border or background around the embroidered design.

Needles

The ideal needle for embroidery should pierce the fabric easily and pull the thread through the fabric smoothly. *Crewel* needles are long and sharp and have large eyes. Size 5 is ideal to use with 6-ply embroidery floss and pearl cotton. *Chenille* needles are also sharp and large-eyed, but are shorter. Size 19 is appropriate for use with 3-ply Persian-type or crewel yarn.

Threads

Embroidery floss: This is a shiny, twisted 6-strand thread. The strands can be separated for doing fine embroidery.

Pearl cotton: This is a smooth, corded thread whose strands cannot be separated.

3-strand Persian-type yarn or crewel yarn: A 3-strand wool or acrylic yarn, each strand made up of 2-ply threads twisted together. For most embroidery, stitch with only one of the three strands at a time.

Fabrics

Natural linen is perhaps the most suitable fabric for most embroidery. Substitutes could be synthetic linen, such as butcher linen (which is made up of rayon fiber), or other loosely woven and strong-threaded fabrics, such as hopsacking and cotton/synthetic blends.

Transferring the Design

First, using tracing paper, trace the desired design motif from the book. Then use any of the following methods to transfer the motif to the fabric:

Draw the Design Right on the Fabric

Place the tracing underneath the fabric and pin the two together. Using masking tape, tape them to a window during daylight. Unless you are using a very dark fabric, the design will show through the fabric. Using a sharp-pointed pencil or pen, draw the design on the fabric.

Use Dressmaker's Carbon Paper

Pin the tracing, at its very top, to the fabric. Slide a sheet of contrasting color carbon paper between the two. Pin together the other three sides. Trace around the design's outlines very heavily with a pencil. Periodically unpin two sides and check the fabric to see that the design is transferring. If not, outline it again, more heavily this time.

Use a Transfer Pencil

Heat-sensitive copying pencils make pink outlines and are available at many craft and art supply stores. Make sure the pencil's point is very sharp. On the *wrong side* of the tracing, draw the outlines of the design, making sure no smudging occurs. Place the tracing on the fabric with the pink side facing the fabric, and pin two sides. Then apply a hot iron to the paper, lifting it every few seconds so as not to scorch the fabric. Pick up the tracing occasionally to see if the design appears clearly on the fabric. If not, apply more heat.

Using an Embroidery Hoop

Most embroidery should be worked on fabric pulled taut by a frame or hoop. Though large projects require square frames, small round hoops, 5″ or 6″ in diameter, are sufficient for the small embroidery projects in this book. The hoop, made of wood, metal, or plastic, consists of two loops, one larger than the other, with a screw for tightening the spring mechanism. The fabric is placed over the smaller hoop, then the larger hoop is pushed over the fabric-covered hoop. The screw is tightened and the excess fabric is pulled all around so that the material within the hoop is very taut.

Starting and Ending the Stitching

The end of the yarn strand is knotted and the needle is brought up from the wrong side. Ending off is done by weaving the needle two or three times through a few stitches on the wrong side of the work.

Mounting and Framing the Embroidery

Purchased frames generally come supplied with a mounting board. You can also make one by cutting a piece of stiff corrugated cardboard or matte board to the dimensions of the frame's back opening. Or you can cut the mounting board to any size you want and then have a frame custom-made to the required dimensions.

Before mounting the embroidered fabric, trim it so it measures 2″ longer and wider than the mounting board. Stretch and fold the fabric over the board and tape down a 1″ hem on two opposing sides, using masking or vinyl tape but not cellophane tape. Fold in and miter each of the four corners and tape down the two remaining sides. Insert the piece into the frame's back opening and tape it to the frame, or hammer small brads all around to keep the board in place.

The same method can be used for mounting needlepointed pieces, patchwork wall decorations, and bargello pictures. For large items use a thicker, stronger cardboard, or wood.

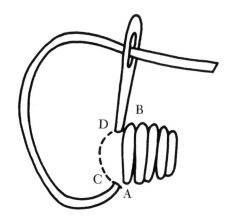

Figure 1

Satin Stitch

Come up at A on outline of the design, go down into fabric at B. Come up at C very close to A, go down at D. Place the stitches close together to cover design area completely (Figure 1). Back of work will be covered with stitches, same as the front.

French Knot

Bring needle up where dot is to be made. Wind thread around point of needle two or three times (Figure 2), then insert it into fabric as close as possible to (but not in exact spot) where yarn was brought up (Figure 3). Pull it to the wrong side, holding twists in place (Figure 4).

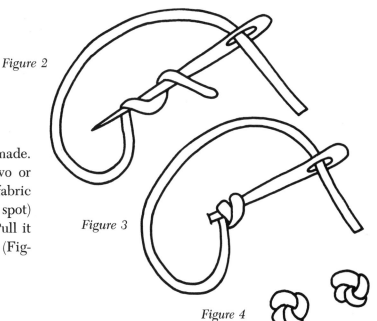

Figure 2

Figure 3

Figure 4

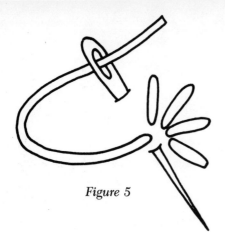

Figure 5

Straight Stitch

The straight stitch consists of single stitches scattered in a pattern to form a flower (Figure 5).

Backstitch

Working from right to left bring the needle up at A, insert it ¼″ behind at B, then come up again ¼″ ahead at C. Draw the needle through (Figure 6).

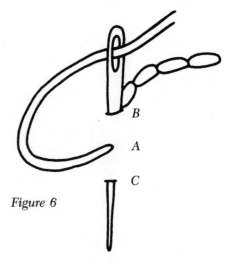

Figure 6

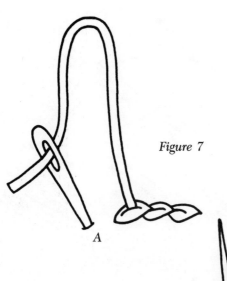

Figure 7

Split Stitch

Bring needle up to right side of fabric. Insert it ¼″ away at A (Figure 7). Come up again at B, piercing through the center of the stitch just made (Figure 8).

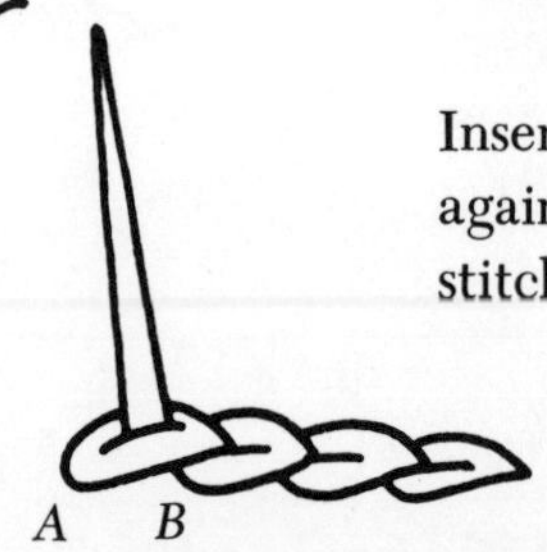

Figure 8

Chain Stitch

Bring the needle to right side of fabric. Reinsert needle where thread emerges and come up ¼″ ahead. While needle is still in fabric, place thread counterclockwise around it (Figure 9). Draw the needle through.

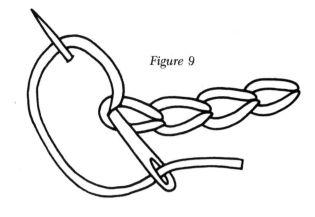

Figure 9

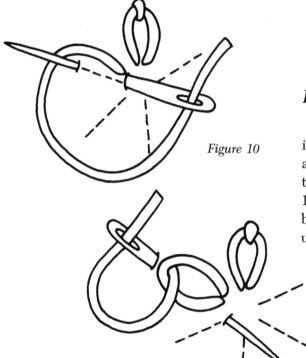

Figure 10

Lazy Daisy Stitch

Bring needle up at bottom of stitch. Insert it again into same hole, then come up ¼″ away. Place thread counterclockwise around the needle and pull the needle through (Figure 10). Fasten the stitch by inserting the needle behind it to form a small straight stitch (Figure 11).

Figure 11

Weaving

Using one color yarn, lay stitches across the design area, placing them the width of one thread apart. Thread a blunt-pointed needle with a contrasting color yarn and weave under and over the other threads, with each row fastened to the fabric at either side (Figure 12). Rows of weaving should be closely spaced so that the woven effect fully covers the fabric.

Figure 12

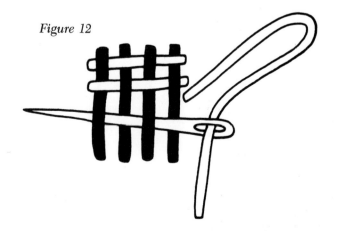

Mirror embroidery, embellished with borders of lazy daisy stitches, straight stitches, and cretan stitches.

Figure 1

Mirror Embroidery

This type of embroidery involves attaching round, flat discs to the fabric without sewing through them. The discs can be $\frac{1}{2}$"- or $\frac{3}{4}$"-diameter mirrors, paillettes (large sequins), or round pieces cut from stiff tinsel. The fabric to sew them to can be linen, cotton, satin, or any other fabric through which you can sew with an embroidery needle. Embroidery floss, which has no resilience and a lustrous texture, makes the most secure and attractive fastening for these discs. In attaching them it is not necessary to use an embroidery hoop.

Thread a needle with 3 strands or all 6 strands of embroidery floss, or 2 strands of pearl cotton. Place the disc on the fabric and secure it with 2 vertical threads, AB and CD (Figure 1). Then come up at E, pull the thread under AB, then under CD and go down at F. Work horizontal thread GH the same way (Figure 2). Work the needle through the back of the disc a few times to fasten this basic framework. With the same color thread come up through the fabric at the edge below the disc. Using the cretan stitch shown in Figure 5, work the top of the stitches into the center of the framework (Figure 3), and the bottom of the stitches into the fabric below the disc, picking up $\frac{1}{8}$" of fabric (Figure 4). Once the framework is covered all around with cretan stitches (Figure 6), work a round of lazy daisy stitches all around for a decorative effect. Or work other stitches around the framework, as shown in the photograph.

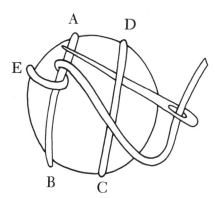

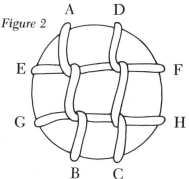

Figure 2

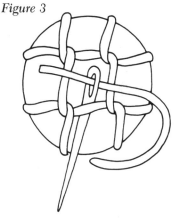

Figure 3

Figure 4

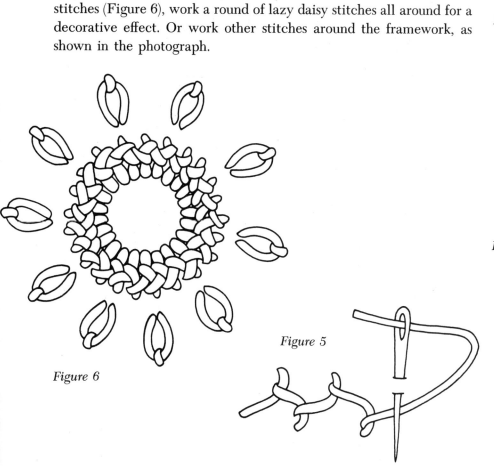

Figure 6

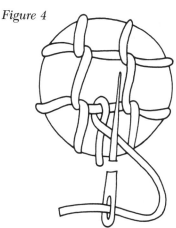

Figure 5

Macrame

MACRAME IS THE craft of knotting rope or other string to make textured patterns. These patterns, in turn, can be formed into useful articles such as wall decorations, household items, and fashion accessories.

Knotting Material

Many yarns, cords, ropes, and twines are suitable for knotting. They should be non-elastic and not too stiff. Butcher twine, rug yarn, jute twine, cable cord (which has a very noticeable twist), and rattail (shiny rayon threads woven around a cotton filler) are some of the materials that can be used for making any of the hanging planters, wall hangings, and jewelry projects in this book. Many of these materials are sold in a natural color only, but you can color them with a commercial dye by immersing a loosely-wrapped and tied skein of any of these into a dye bath, following instructions on the package.

Estimating Yardages

Specific yardages for completing the item are indicated for each project. If you wish to make an item longer, for example, extending a wall-hanging strip into a ceiling-to-floor room divider—use the following formula for estimating yardages:

Each working strand should be 4 times the length of the finished project. If the strand is folded in half and mounted on a dowel, then it should be cut 8 times the finished length. For example, if you wish to make a wall-hanging 2 yards long, each strand should be cut 16 yards long. When folded in half and mounted on a dowel, each cut strand would yield 2 working strands, each 8 yards long. When knotted, the strip would be 2 yards long.

Knotting Board and Pins

The knots of macrame are worked while all the strands are securely pinned to a special knotting board. The board can be an 18″ by 24″ piece of Celotex or Upson board, available at lumber yards. Or it can be a combination of materials, available at art supply stores under the trade name Foam-Core; this consists of a sheet of plastic foam sandwiched between two sheets of heavy paper. In addition, many craft stores carry special macrame boards which are printed with a 1″ grid for more even placement of the knots.

The pins are used for holding the strands on the board as you are making the knots. They can be push pins, T-pins, or dressmaker pins.

The photograph shows the proper sitting position for working macrame. Sit in a chair, with the board resting in your lap and leaning against a table.

Beads

A variety of colorful and unusual glass, wood, or clay beads are available if you wish to insert them between macrame knots for a more decorative look. You could also make beads yourself out of papier-mâché or self-hardening clay, both available at art supply stores. In purchasing or making beads, be sure the holes are large enough for two strands of cord to pass through. To help in inserting the strand through the bead, place a piece of tape around the end of the strand to form a point.

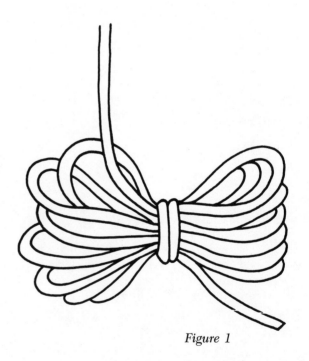

Figure 1

Working with Long Strands

When making large items such as room dividers and wall hangings, the strands may be too long to knot easily. Each strand can be made shorter by winding it over the palm of the hand to a more convenient length and securing it with a rubber band (Figure 1).

Holding Cord

Many of the macrame projects involve mounting strands on a dowel, ring, or cord. To form a holding cord out of string, make an overhand knot, as shown in Figure 2, on either side of the string, making the two knots about 10″ apart. Pin each knot to the board (Figure 3), with the pins inserted toward the center for more tension (Figure 4).

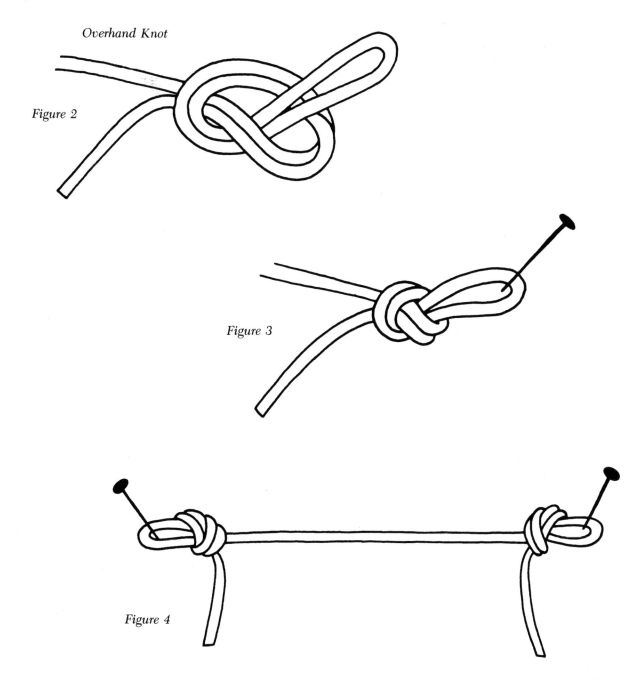

Overhand Knot

Figure 2

Figure 3

Figure 4

Anchor Cord and Knotting Cord

In any macrame knot, each strand has a function. The *anchor cord* serves as a base and is knotted over with the other strand or strands; the *knotting cord* is the strand that is doing the knotting over the *anchor cord* (Figure 5). The cords' functions do not necessarily remain constant. In making the next knot of the pattern the *anchor cord* could become a *knotting cord,* and the *knotting cord* could become an *anchor cord.*

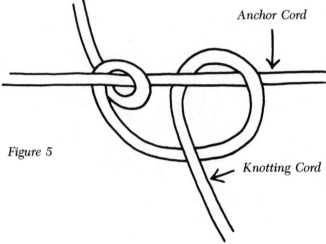

Figure 5

Mounting Strands with a Lark's Head Knot

Fold the strand in half and place the fold over the dowel or holding cord (Figure 6).

Fold the loop over and behind the holding cord (Figure 7).

Place the two ends through the loop (Figure 8).

Pull the ends to tighten the knot. Insert a pin into the top of the knot to secure the strands to the board (Figure 9).

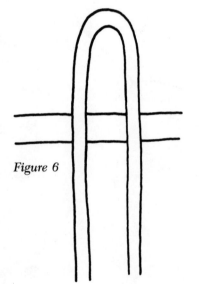

Figure 6

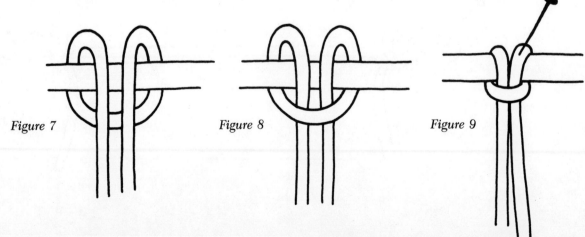

Figure 7   *Figure 8*   *Figure 9*

The Square Knot

Place A over center strands, under B (Figure 10).

Place B under A and center strands; pull it out over A on left side (Figure 11).

Place B under center strands, over A (Figure 12).

Place A over center strands, through loop formed by B on left side (Figure 13).

Tighten knot by pulling A and B (Figure 14).

Figure 10

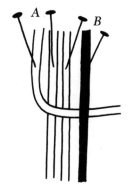

Figure 11

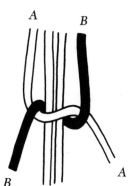

Figure 12

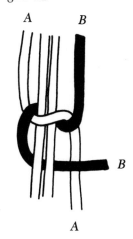

Figure 13

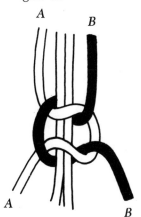

Figure 14

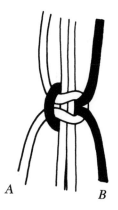

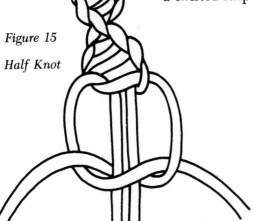

The Half Knot

Working over 1 or 2 anchor cords, make the first half of the square knot and continue to work consecutive half knots close together to form a twisted strip (Figure 15).

Figure 15

Half Knot

Alternating Square Knot

This pattern requires an even number of strands. Work a square knot on each group of 4 strands, knotting over 2 anchor cords. On the second row, knot with the anchor cords, using the previous row's knotting cords as the anchor cords. There will be two unknotted strands on either side, and one less square knot on the second row. The third row is identical to the first (Figure 16).

Figure 16

Alternating Square Knot

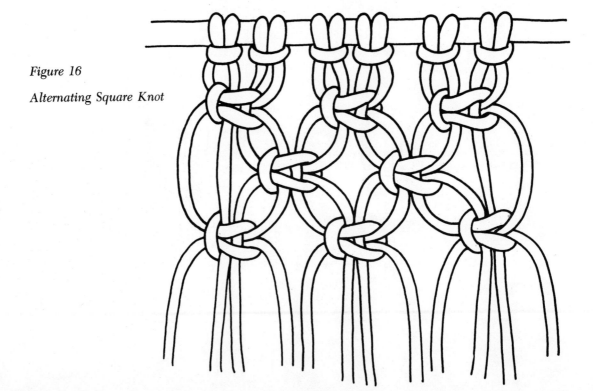

Horizontal Double Half Hitch Knot

Pin the anchor cord tautly across the knotting cords. Starting with the first strand at left, place it over the anchor cord once and then over again as shown (Figure 17), forming a double half hitch knot. Make a double half hitch knot with each strand across, from left to right. Horizontal double half hitch knots could also be worked from right to left, as shown in Figure 18, or diagonally, when the anchor cord is pinned across the strands diagonally.

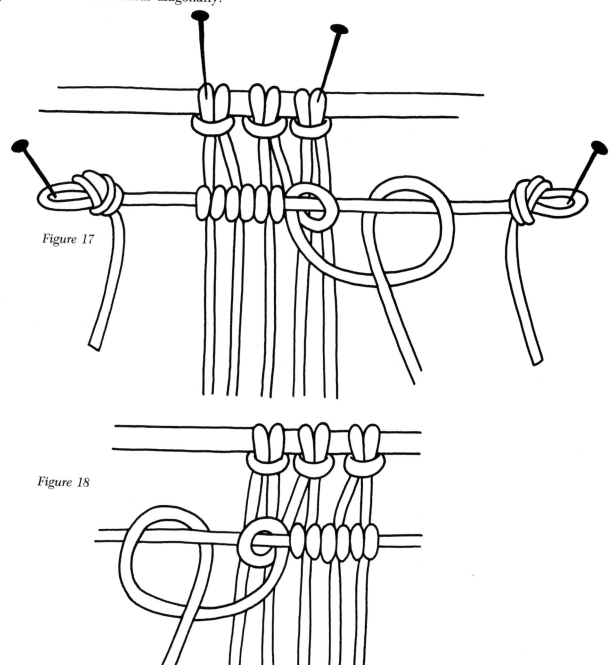

Figure 17

Figure 18

Alternating Double Half Hitch Knot

This knot is worked with only 2 strands. With A, make a double half hitch knot over B, then make a double half hitch knot with B over A. Alternate in this manner (Figure 19).

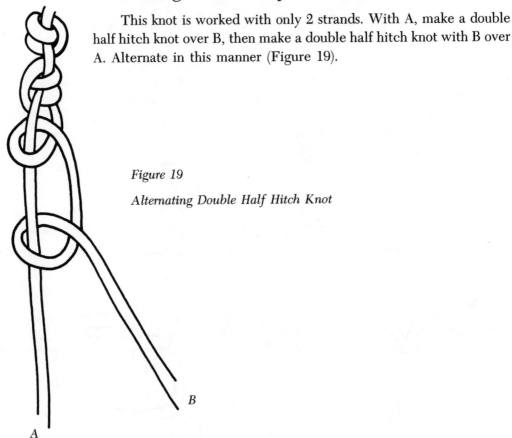

Figure 19

Alternating Double Half Hitch Knot

The Wrapped Knot

Shown in the illustrations is a wrapped knot being made to tie together the two sides of a knotted loop hanger, shown in the Double-Decker Hanging Planter in chapter 4. A wrapped knot can also be made to tie together the strands at the bottom of a hanging planter, the strands at the bottom of a macrame hanging, and the strands at the two ends of a macramed sash.

Place a wrapping strand over all the strands, forming loop B and making sure A will extend above the knot (Figure 20). Wrap end C around all the strands very tightly, about 10 or 12 times. Insert end C through loop B (Figure 21). Pull end A so that the loop disappears under the knot. Clip off ends A and C close to the knot (Figure 22).

The Wrapped Knot

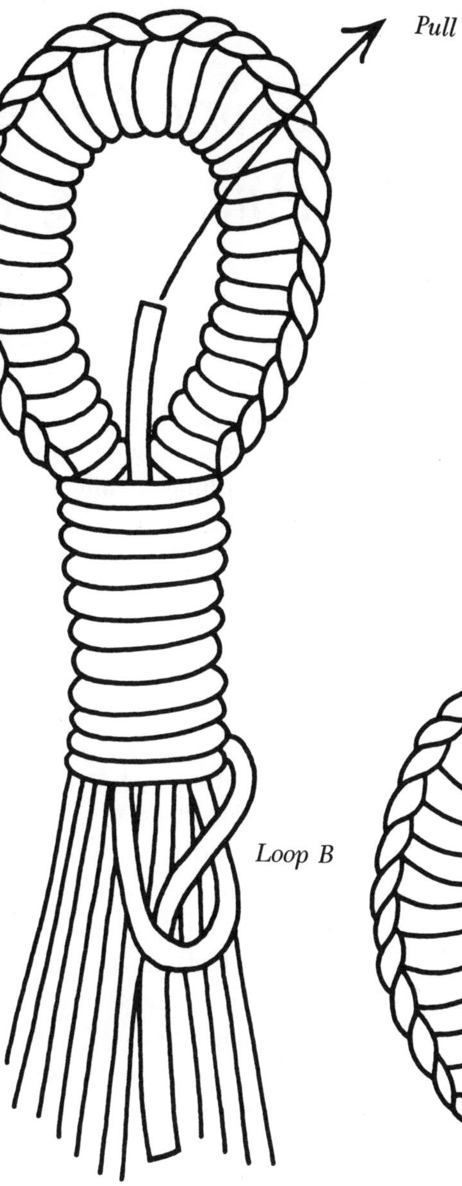

Figure 21

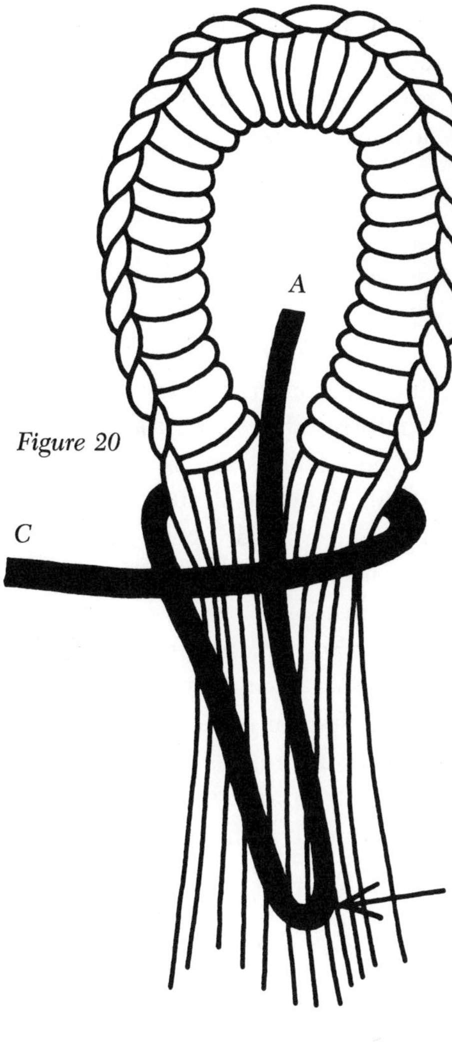

Pull

Figure 20

A

C

Loop B

Loop B

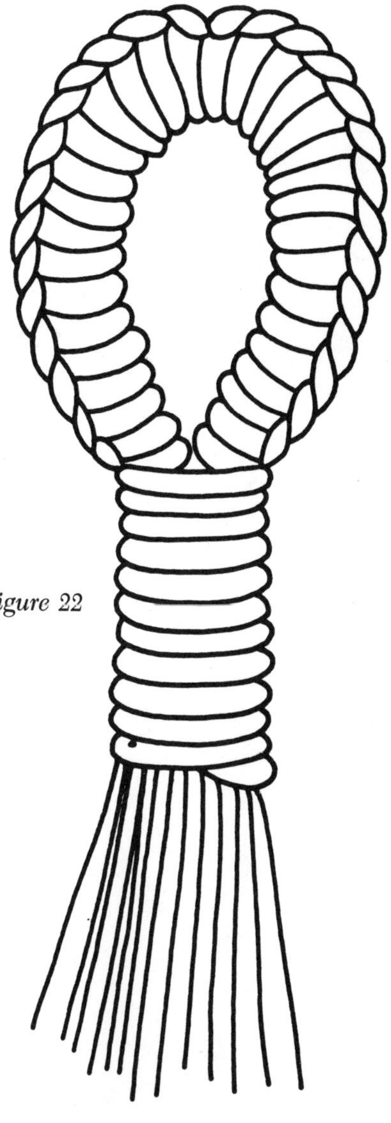

Figure 22

Fabric Crafts: Appliqué, Patchwork, and Quilting

WHILE LARGE PIECES of fabric can be sewn into garments and home furnishings items, the variety of prints and solids left over from these projects can be utilized by making them into charming, handcrafted accessories. Appliqué and patchwork are methods of combining pieces of fabric together, each achieving a distinct decorative effect. Quilting is a finishing technique, and serves as one method by which patch-worked and appliquéd fabrics are made into completed items.

Fabrics

For any of these crafts, it is important to choose the proper materials. Certain fabrics are more suitable than others for cutting apart and sewing together. The best fabrics are smooth, soft, non-ravelling, and colorfast, with a firm weave. Cottons—whether solid, gingham, or printed with a calico pattern— are best. Flannel, satin, silk, velvet, velveteen, wool, and corduroy are also worth considering, especially for sewing into patchwork patterns. It is important to combine fabrics properly, for esthetic and practical reasons. Washable cottons should not be sewn to non-washable satins and velvets. Try, too, to combine fabrics of similar weight, especially when doing patchwork; thin voile should not be sewn to heavy denim, nor fine taffeta attached to woolens. If you are using cottons, try to pre-shrink all the fabrics, especially if you intend to machine-wash rather than dry-clean the item later.

Other materials you may require for fabric crafts are batting for quilting and fusible webbing for iron-on appliqué. Both these products are widely available in fabric and department stores. Batting is a puffy, non-woven sheeting which comes in varying thicknesses and widths. The preferred type is made from polyester fibers; the traditional kind is made from cotton. Fusible webbing for appliqué is packaged under several brand names. It is sold by the yard in narrow widths, as well as in strips ½″ and 1″ wide, and is accompanied by full instructions for use.

Making a Template

Using tracing or tissue paper, trace the pattern from the book on the cutting line. Glue the tracing to cardboard or a file folder. When dry, cut out the pattern on the cutting line.

Marking the Pattern

Place the template on the fabric, making sure the grain line on the pattern is parallel to the selvage of the fabric. Holding the template down, outline it all around with a pen or pencil (Figure 1). Cut out the fabric piece.

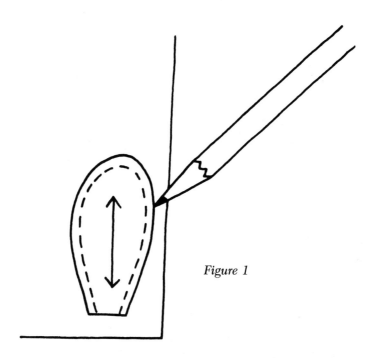

Figure 1

Appliqué

APPLIQUÉ IS THE craft of overlaying and attaching decoratively shaped pieces of material onto another fabric. There are two basic ways of appliquéing the pieces. The more time-consuming method involves hemming them down with small, almost invisible stitches. The other method, very useful in creating hand-crafted items in a minimum period of time, employs a special bonding medium which is placed under the appliqué and causes it to adhere to the backing fabric when melted by a hot iron. Most woven fabrics can be appliquéd by either of these methods. Felt, since it is a non-woven fabric and does not ravel, can be either fused on, glued on with white glue, or simply applied with a running stitch around the edges.

Turned-Edge Appliqué

Cut out the appliqué with ¼″ seam allowance all around. Machine stitch ¼″ in from the edge. Clip the seam allowance all around, up to the stitching line, as shown in Figure 2. Turn the ¼″ edge to the wrong side; using the machine stitches as a guide, pin the appliqué to the backing and stitch it in place with small stitches. If you wish, you can use a running stitch close to the edge instead.

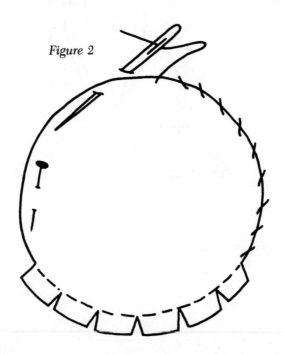

Figure 2

Iron-On Appliqué

Cut out the appliqué without any seam allowance. Cut out a piece of exact size and shape from fusible webbing. Place the webbing on the backing fabric and place the appliqué on top of it (Figure 3). Follow instructions accompanying the fusible webbing and fuse the appliqué to the backing by placing a hot iron on top of it for a few seconds. Be careful not to scorch the fabric.

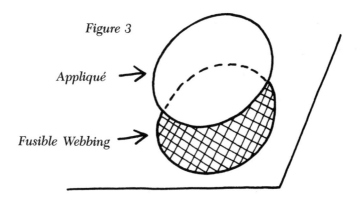

Figure 3

Appliqué →

Fusible Webbing →

Edge the appliqué by either of the two following methods:

Machine Zigzagging

Have the stitches $\frac{1}{4}''$ wide, $\frac{1}{16}''$ apart (not tightly worked as for buttonholes). Do the stitching so that it falls mainly on the appliqué, not half on the appliqué and half on the backing (Figure 4). Later, steam press the piece to flatten any buckling caused by the stitching.

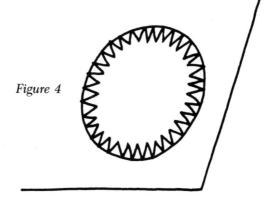

Figure 4

Blanket Stitch Embroidery

Use 3 strands of 6-strand embroidery floss, in a matching or contrasting color. Come up at A. Insert needle at B, $\frac{1}{4}''$ in from the edge of the appliqué. Come up again at C, beyond the appliqué's edge. Place the thread behind the needle and pull the needle out (Figure 5). Follow these steps and work even stitches all around, adjusting the angle of the stitches to follow the shape of the appliqué.

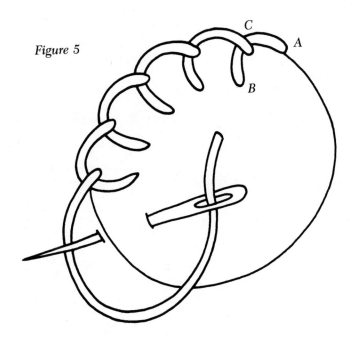

Figure 5

Patchwork

PATCHWORK IS THE craft of sewing together geometric, or odd-shaped, pieces of fabric to form a large, patterned length of material. The patchwork hangings on page 150 feature traditional patterns made from squares and triangles. If your fabric scraps are not large enough to be made into these attractive hangings, make them into crazy-quilt patterned pot holders, placemats, and wooden-handled bags.

Crazy-Quilt Patchwork

Use a piece of batiste or muslin as a backing. Cut out odd-shaped angular pieces of calicoes, ginghams, and solids. Place one on top of the other, overlapping them at least ½″ so that the backing will not show through (Figure 6). Pin, and baste the pieces down. Then, either machine zigzag all the raw edges, or work the herringbone stitch on each edge, as shown in Figure 7, using three strands of six-strand embroidery floss. Trim the edges of the piece all around to even them out.

Herringbone Stitch

Figure 6

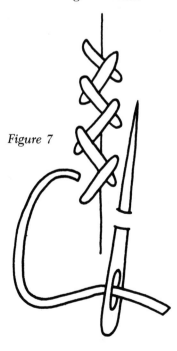

Figure 7

Quilting

QUILTING IS THE technique of attaching a decorated top layer of fabric to a plain bottom layer, with a puffy layer of batting sandwiched between the two. This is done by sewing through all three layers at once. The stitching can be done either by hand (working small basting stitches with strong mercerized thread), or by straight machine sewing. Though the stitching on large quilts is often done in patterned rows creating fascinating textural effects, the quilted projects in this book call for stitching around appliquéd motifs or on seam lines, as for the floral patterned mini-quilt.

Large quilts, stitched by hand, require the use of a quilting frame. The small quilted projects presented here do not. The technique of preparing the three layers for quilting is the same.

Lay the backing on a flat surface, wrong side up. Place the polyester or cotton batting on top of it and smooth it out. Then place the top of the quilt, right side up, over the batting. Next, insert many pins all over, smoothing out all three layers. Check to see that there are no wrinkles. Baste the three layers together in rows, 4″ or 5″ apart, down the length of the quilt. Do the same across. Then stitch through all three layers, by machine or by hand, working around appliqués, on seam lines, or on the outlines of a boldly printed top fabric. When done, trim the edges all around so all layers line up evenly. Finish the edges by sewing commercial bias binding around them, or with bias strips cut from a print fabric, following the technique shown for the miniature quilt in chapter 5.

Quilting can be used for making attractive pot holders, placemats, and fabric bags, and wall hangings, using any of the patchwork designs in chapter 5.

Crochet

CROCHET IS THE craft of forming fabric by looping yarn with a crochet hook. It is just about the speediest needlecraft technique, requiring very few materials—a crochet hook and yarn. Though an unlimited variety of stitches, combinations of stitches, and patterns exist in crochet, it is possible to make many attractive household and fashion items with a knowledge of only two or three simple stitches.

Hooks and Yarns

Crochet hooks come in a variety of sizes, each designed for use with a different weight of yarn. The fine steel hooks, ranging in size from 14 (the finest) to 00 (the largest), are used for crocheting with crochet cotton, and other fine yarns. Aluminum and plastic hooks, with C the finest and K the largest, are used for crocheting with wool, synthetic, and novelty yarns.

Most of the crochet projects in this book are designed to be made in any texture, or weight, of yarn. The same item, say the mesh shawl, can be crocheted in a heavy yarn such as rug yarn, or in as thin a yarn as fine crochet cotton. Of course, the heavier the yarn used, the faster the project can be completed.

Before beginning any crochet project it is essential to crochet a 3″ wide sample swatch in double crochet stitch, making about four or five rows. Use the following chart to determine which hook to use with your choice of yarn. Make a sample in each hook size given for that yarn and try to match the best gauge as indicated in the chart, or the gauge specified in the instructions for the item. When crocheting with a combination of yarns, such as two strands of metallic yarn, or one strand of mohair with one strand of worsted yarn, use a much larger hook than the one specified for only one strand of that yarn. Keep in mind that crocheted fabric should be soft and pliant, not stiff and boardy.

Gauge

To arrive at the gauge, or measurements, of a crocheted sample, simply measure it horizontally to determine how many stitches there are in a one-inch or two-inch space, and vertically, to find how many rows measure one or two inches (Figure 1). If there are too many

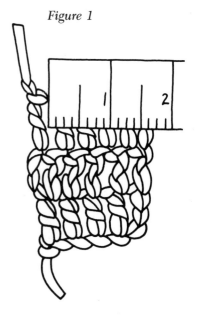

Figure 1

45

stitches and/or rows in one inch, try crocheting with a larger hook. If there are too few stitches and/or rows per inch, then use a smaller hook.

Yarn and Crochet Hook Chart

Type of Yarn	Description of Yarn	Hook to Use	Best Gauge for Crochet
worsted yarn	4-ply wool, or acrylic, yarn	G, H, or I aluminum	4 dc sts = 1″ 2 dc rows = 1″
sport yarn	2- or 3-ply wool, or acrylic; finer than worsted yarn	E, F, or G aluminum	6 dc sts = 1″ 3 dc rows = 2″
rug yarn, bulky yarn	3-ply wool, acrylic, or cotton yarn; heavier than worsted yarn	J or K aluminum	5 dc sts = 2″ 2 dc rows = 1½″
metallic yarn, crepe yarn, bouclé yarn	novelty textured yarns, made up of different fibers; usually finer than worsted yarn	E, F, or G aluminum	6 dc sts = 1″ 3 dc rows = 2″
fine crochet cotton	very thin, non-elastic cotton yarn; used for doilies	6, 5, 4, and 3 steel hook	8 dc sts = 1″ 4 dc rows = 1″
medium-weight crochet cotton	slightly heavier, and stiffer, non-elastic cotton	2, 1, 0, and 00 steel hook	11 dc sts = 2″ 4 dc rows = 1½″
butcher twine	multi-ply cotton string; used for wrapping packages	I, J, or K aluminum	5 dc sts = 2″ 2 dc rows = 1½″
rayon rattail	shiny rayon fibers around a cotton filler; used for macrame	I, J, or K aluminum	5 dc sts = 2″ 2 dc rows = 1½″
jute twine	ropelike yarn, usually 2-ply; made of jute	J or K aluminum	5 dc sts = 2″ 2 dc rows = 1½″
raffia, synthetic straw	flat yarn, non-elastic	H, I, or J aluminum	7 dc sts = 2″ 2 dc rows = 1¼″

Estimating Yarn Amounts

Yarn amount specifications are indicated for each crochet project. Yarn amounts given are for specific projects and exact size duplication. If you make a different size or vary the specifications (choose a different yarn or hook, for example), the yardage will change accordingly.

The amount of yarn you need will depend on how large an item you wish to make. For example, if you want to make a crocheted covering for a lampshade that is larger than the one shown in chapter 3, you will require more yarn than is specified. Accurate yarn amounts are not indicated for the wall hanging with crocheted appliqués, in chapter 5, because the amount you need will depend on how large the hanging is to be.

Listed for each project is a choice of yarns you can use, each a different weight and texture. Each yarn type has a different yardage count. For example, an ounce of rug yarn has fewer yards than an ounce of crochet cotton.

It is always a good idea to buy more yarn than is specified, making sure the skeins are all of the same dye lot. Many knitting stores accept returns of skeins that are unused. Or, unused yarn can be utilized for smaller items.

Blocking a Finished Project

When a project has been completed, it should be smoothed and flattened with a light steam pressing. Undesirable puffiness of the surface can usually be corrected by blocking. To block, place the item on an ironing board. Saturate a paper towel or a press cloth with water, wring it out, and place it flat on the item. Hold a hot iron lightly on top of the paper towel or press cloth. A hissing sound will result. Make sure the iron does not rest its weight directly on top of the crocheted work. Heavy pressing results in a very flat texture, permanently spoiling an attractive surface. Let the steamed area dry. Then repeat the process on other areas of the project.

Crochet Language and How to Read It

SINCE MOST CROCHET stitches have lengthy names, crochet directions are written in a shorthand language. The shorthand is an abbreviation of the stitch name. The following are the standard crochet abbreviations and their meanings.

sp(s)	space(s)	trc	triple crochet
ch	chain	dtrc	double triple crochet
ch st	chain stitch	yo	yarn over (hook)
sl st	slip stitch	sk	skip
sc	single crochet	beg	beginning
st	stitch	dec	decrease
sts	stitches	inc	increase
hdc	half double crochet	tog	together
dc	double crochet		

In addition to abbreviations of stitch names, crochet language includes the following symbols:

Asterisk: The asterisk (*) serves as a marker in a row or round of stitches. When you are told to "repeat from * 4 times," for example, you work the specified stitches the first time. Then you return to the * and repeat what is written after it, four times.

Parentheses: One function of parentheses is to enclose a number of stitches which must all be worked into one space or stitch.

example: (3 dc, ch 3, 3 dc) in corner ch-3 sp

That means that you must work three double crochet stitches, chain 3, and three more double crochet stitches into the chain 3 space at the corner of a square. Other times, parentheses enclose instructions for stitches to be done several times.

Example: (dc, ch 2) 11 times into ring.

That means that you must work a double crochet stitch, followed by chain 2, eleven times into the ring. In other words, do what is in the parentheses the specified number of times.

48

Basic Knots, Chains, and Stitches

The Slip Knot

All crocheting begins with the slip knot. It is the first loop you place on the hook. Once the slip knot is in place, you chain a group of stitches which will become the foundation for your crochet pattern.

Working on a flat surface, hold cut end of yarn B and form it into a circle (Figure 2). Place end A across the circle, cutting circle in half (Figure 3). Pull center strand up through circle with one hand, while grasping ends A and B with the other hand (Figure 4). A knot will form (Figure 5).

Insert hook into loop and pull end A so that loop becomes smaller and conforms to the size of the hook. Hook should be held as you would hold a dinner knife (Figure 6).

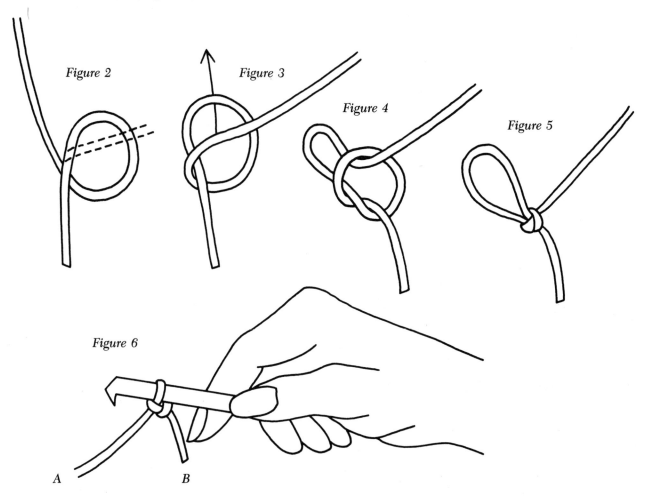

Figure 2

Figure 3

Figure 4

Figure 5

Figure 6

A   B

Holding Hook and Yarn

Grasp end B with thumb and index finger of left hand, while raising left forefinger. Yarn is draped over forefinger, while pinky and ring fingers are folded over towards palm. These two fingers serve as a tension spool, as on a sewing machine. By resting against the yarn loosely, they perpetually loosen and tighten their hold on the yarn as it passes through the left hand. Allowing the yarn a proper, even tension is a skill that must be developed through practice. The tighter the hold of these two fingers on the yarn, the smaller and tighter the stitches. The tightness or looseness of the stitches also depends on the weight of the yarn, the hook size, and even your degree of relaxation when you crochet.

The Chain (ch)

Make a slip knot. To begin chaining, pass hook *under* the yarn and catch it with the hook. Pull the yarn back through the loop on the hook. What is formed is a first chain (ch). Passing the hook under the yarn is called yarn over (yo). Repeat this chaining process of yarn over and pulling loop through last chain as many times as the number of chains you require (Figure 7). The knot *does not* count as a chain.

As you complete four or five chains, move the thumb and index finger further up the chain towards the hook for better control of the work. Be sure the chaining row remains even and symmetrical, with a series of Vs, one coming out of the other.

Figure 7

The Slip Stitch (sl st)

The slip stitch is used mainly to join rounds of crocheting together. It has no height and cannot be worked in rows, or rounds, like all the other stitches.

Insert hook in chain, yarn over, and pull a loop through the chain (Figure 8). Pull new loop through old loop on hook.

Figure 8

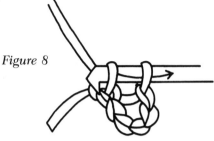

The Single Crochet Stitch (sc)

To practice, begin with a chain of 15 stitches. Insert hook in second chain from hook, yarn over, and pull a loop through the chain (Figure 9). Yarn over again and pull new loop through two loops on hook (Figure 10). Work a single crochet stitch in every chain across. At end of row, chain 1 (Figure 11). Turn piece.

Row 2: Single crochet in every sc stitch across. Chain 1, turn. Repeat Row 2 for consecutive rows of single crochet.

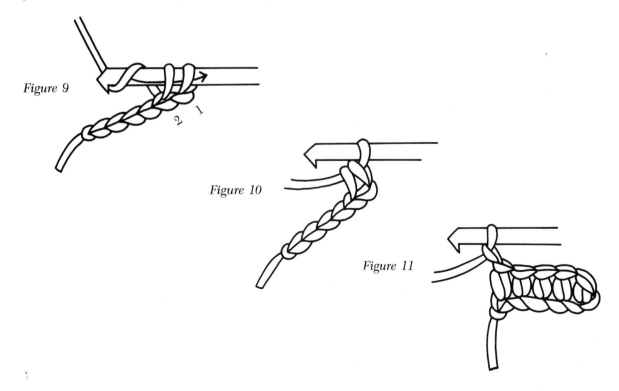

Figure 9

Figure 10

Figure 11

To Increase 1 SC ST

Work 2 single crochet stitches in one stitch.

To Decrease 1 SC ST

Figure 12

Pull a loop through first stitch. Then pull a loop through next stitch. Yarn over and pull yarn through all three loops on hook (Figure 12).

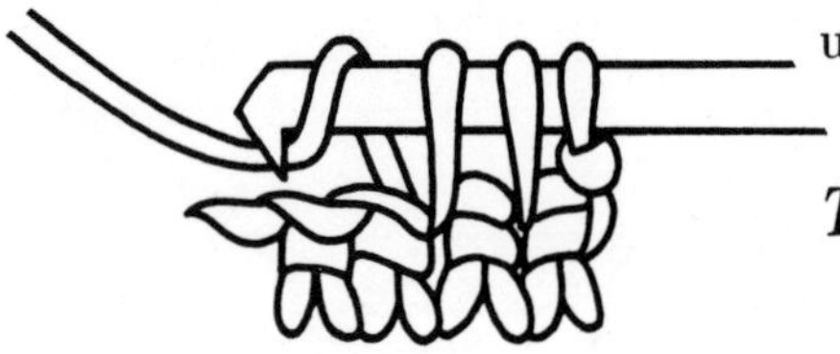

The Half Double Crochet Stitch (hdc)

To practice, begin with a chain of 15 stitches. Yarn over hook once (Figure 13). Insert hook in third chain from hook, yarn over, and pull a loop through chain (Figure 14). Yarn over and pull yarn through all three loops on hook (Figure 15). Work a half double crochet stitch in next chain and every chain across. Chain 2 (Figure 16). Turn.

Row 2: Half double crochet in first stitch and every stitch across. Chain 2, turn.

Repeat Row 2 for consecutive rows.

Figure 13

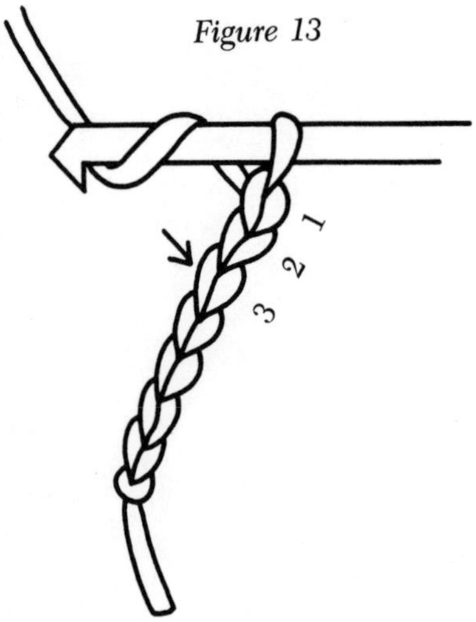

Figure 14

Figure 15

Figure 16

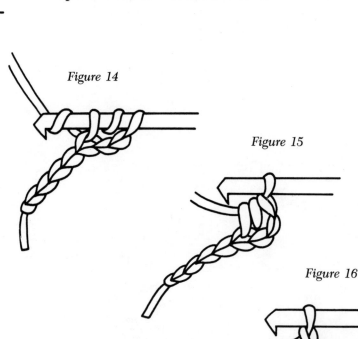

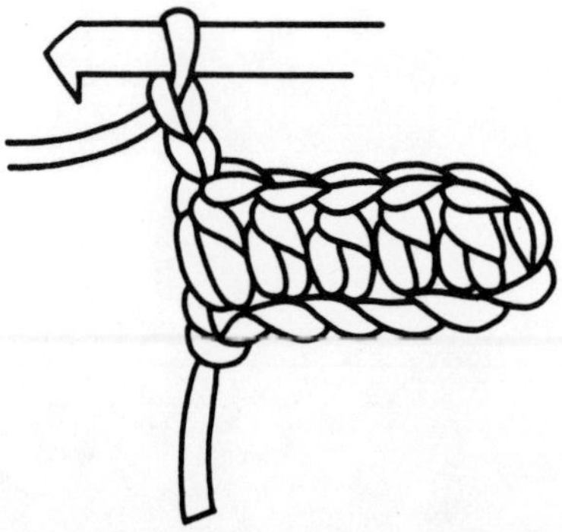

The Double Crochet Stitch (dc)

To practice, begin with a chain of 15 stitches. Yarn over hook once (Figure 17). Insert hook in fourth chain from hook, yarn over, and pull a loop through the chain (Figure 18). Yarn over and pull yarn through two loops on hook (Figure 19). Yarn over and pull yarn through last two loops on hook (Figure 20). Work a double crochet stitch in next chain and every chain across. Chain 2 (Figure 21). Turn.

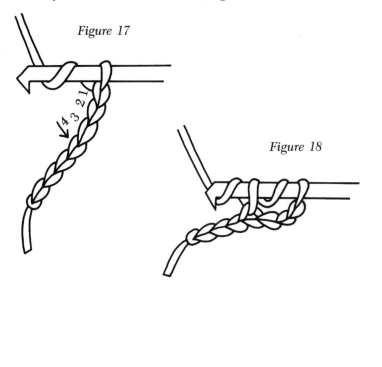

Figure 17

Figure 18

Figure 19

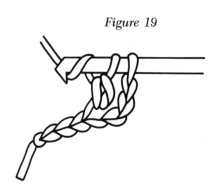

Figure 20

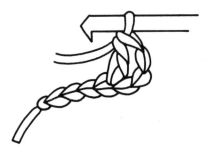

Figure 21

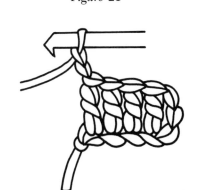

Row 2: Double crochet in top of first stitch, picking up both loops of stitch; double crochet in every stitch across. Work double crochet in third chain of the chain-3 at end of row (Figure 22). Chain 2, turn. (The chain-3 counts as one double crochet stitch.)

Row 3: Double crochet in every stitch across. Chain 2, turn (Figure 23).

Repeat Row 3 for consecutive rows of double crochet stitch.

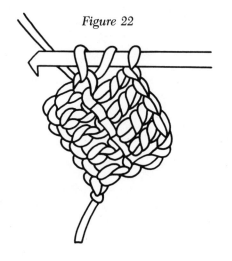

Figure 22

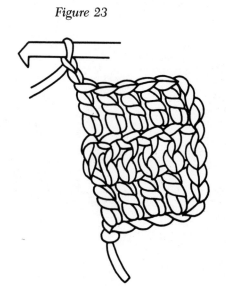

Figure 23

To Increase 1 DC ST

Work 2 double crochet stitches in one stitch (Figure 24).

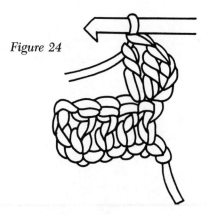

Figure 24

To Decrease 1 DC ST

Yarn over, pull a loop through first stitch, yarn over, and pull yarn through 2 loops on hook; yarn over and pull a loop through next stitch, yarn over, and pull through two loops on hook. Yarn over and pull through all 3 loops on hook (Figure 25).

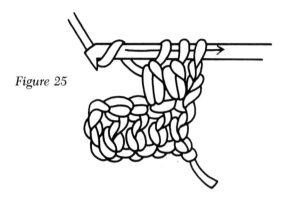

Figure 25

The Triple Crochet Stitch (trc)

To practice, begin with a chain of 15 stitches. Yarn over hook twice (Figure 26). Insert hook in fifth chain from hook, yarn over, and pull a loop through chain, * yarn over and pull yarn through two loops on hook; repeat from * 2 more times (Figure 27). Work a triple crochet stitch in next chain and every chain across. Chain 3 to turn.

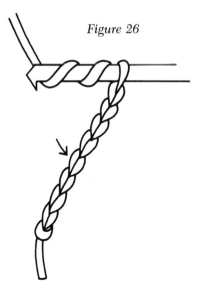

Figure 26

Figure 27

Fastening off

Fastening off, or cutting the yarn, is done at the end of a row or round, wherever specified in the instructions. After working the last stitch of the row, or after joining together the beginning and the end of a round, chain 1. Cut yarn, leaving at least a 3-inch end (Figure 28). Enlarge loop by pulling hook away from work until cut end comes through the chain-1 loop. Pull cut end to tighten the chain-1 into a knot (Figure 29).

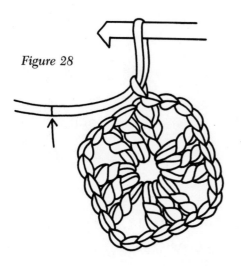

Figure 28

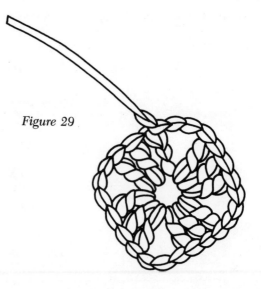

Figure 29

Weaving Ends Through Back of Work

All cut ends of yarn hanging from a crocheted piece must be woven into the wrong side so that the piece will have a neat, clean look. Thread the cut end of yarn into a large-eyed tapestry needle. On back of work, run the needle once through the top loops of two or three stitches (Figure 30), then again through other stitches but in the opposite direction. Cut leftover end close to work. Wrong side of work will look as neat as the right side. This weaving must be done with all yarn ends.

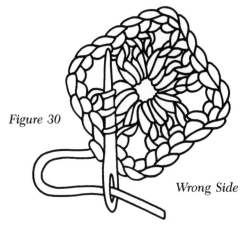

Figure 30

Wrong Side

Changing Colors

Changing Colors in the Middle or End of a Row

In Color A, yarn over and pull a loop through next chain or stitch, yarn over and pull yarn through 2 loops on hook; cut Color A. Pull Color B through remaining 2 loops on hook (Figure 31).

Figure 31

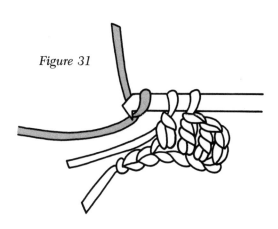

Attaching New Color Yarn When Working in Rounds

Method 1: Insert end of new yarn color through space where second round is to begin. (If new color should be attached in a stitch, use a crochet hook or thread the end into a tapestry needle and use it to pull the end through.) Make a simple knot, tying on the end (Figure 32). Tighten knot, leaving a 3 inch end, and have knot fall at far right corner of space. Insert hook into space and pull through a loop (Figure 33). Proceed, working the next round.

Method 2: Make a slip knot in the new color, leaving a 3 inch end. Insert hook into loop, then insert hook into specified space or stitch and pull through another loop (Figure 34). Work a slip stitch, pulling new loop through original loop on hook. Proceed, working next round.

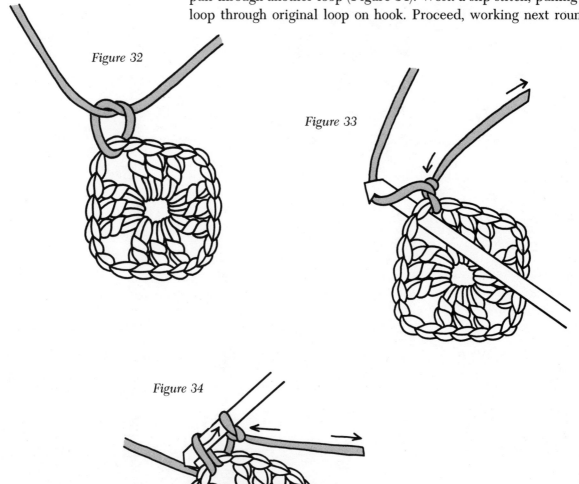

Figure 32

Figure 33

Figure 34

Fringe Edging

Wind yarn around a cardboard gauge, which, when folded, is the desired size of the completed fringe, say 6 inches. Cut yarn at one side (Figure 35). Fold 3 or 4 strands in half. Insert hook in stitch and pull the fold through the stitch (Figure 36). Pull the 6 strands completely through the fold (Figure 37). Pull the 6 strands away from the edge to tighten the knot. Skip the next stitch or two and insert fringe in the following stitch.

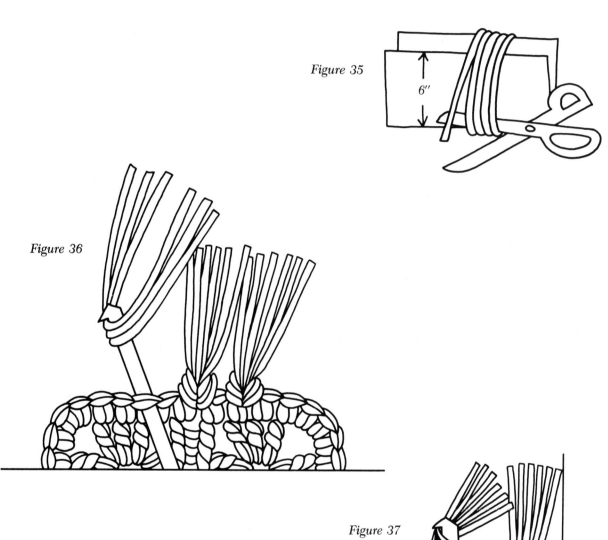

Figure 35

Figure 36

Figure 37

Fashion Accessories ══════════ 2

Whatever your style of dressing may be, you will find a number of ideas in this chapter that can help enhance your wardrobe. Featured is a collection of useful accessories: three hats, two shawls, and a variety of belts, bags, and jewelry. Shown, too, are ways you can trim your old, out-of-style garments, or new, simple clothes with crafts.

Depending on the material you use, each accessory item can be either casual, sophisticated, or formal. Done in bright, happy colors, many of the accessories will delight any little girl or young teen.

The projects are all easy to do and can be handled by anyone with basic skills in the craft. You, as well as your family, will enjoy making, wearing, and giving these unique and useful fashion accessories.

Bags

Wooden–Handled Fabric Bag

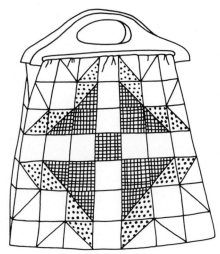

Figure 1

Figure 2

BAGS AND TOTES can be created in any number of craft techniques—crochet, needlepoint, macrame, leathercraft. The simplest and speediest bag to produce is a fabric bag with wooden handles.

The construction is relatively simple. Two rectangles, one for the outside of the bag and the other for the lining, are stitched separately. They are then joined together and attached to either knitting bag handles or wooden dowels. Any kind of fabric—burlap, cotton, linen, felt, vinyl, etc.—can be used to make a simple, wooden-handled bag.

Various craft techniques can be employed to make a fabric bag even more attractive and unusual. One possibility is to quilt a colorful floral or geometric print rectangle, stitching along the outlines of the print. Another version could be made entirely from cut pieces of fabric, either in a crazy-quilt pattern or in any of the patchwork designs appearing in chapter 5. (The crazy-quilt bag is shown in color plate 1.)

Appliquéing the bag is one very simple way to decorate it. You can utilize any of the appliqué designs featured in other projects—the crocheted flower appliqués for the wall hanging in chapter 5, the crocheted flower for the brimmed hat later in this chapter, or the fabric floral motif for the pot holder in chapter 3.

Using embroidery trim is another way to create a unique bag handcrafted from a solid color fabric. The floral stitchery or any of the other mini-stitcheries in chapter 5 can serve as interesting accents. A large muslin or hopsacking bag, with mirror embroidery in an overall pattern as shown in Figure 4, would make a perfect carryall for daytime use. The same mirror stitchery, when applied to a smaller satin or velveteen bag with appropriately smaller handles, would produce a formal evening bag. Instruction for doing the mirror embroidery appear in chapter 1.

If you enjoy challenges and have ample time, you may wish to cut the outer rectangle of the bag out of needlepoint canvas and work the entire surface in a bargello pattern. Remember to leave a $1/2''$-edge of unworked canvas all around for the seam allowance. A simpler and also very effective use of bargello would be to decorate the fabric with bargello strips (Figure 5), made from the belt pattern in this chapter. Or you could decorate the bag with square or rectangular bargello appliqués, using any of the patterns pictured in chapter 1, and sewing them to the bag in the same technique as attaching an appliqué to a pillow, explained in chapter 3.

Whichever of these techniques you choose, be sure to do the needlework on the rectangle before sewing it into a bag. It is easier to work on a flat piece of fabric without interference of bulky handles. The lining you later attach will cover the wrong side of the needlework, providing a clean professional look inside the bag.

Figure 3

Figure 4

Figure 5

How to Make the Fabric Bag

MATERIALS:

18″ x 32″ piece of cotton, linen, burlap, felt, velveteen, or desired fabric for outside of bag

18″ x 32″ piece of batiste, taffeta, or satin for the lining

wood or plastic knitting bag handles with 11″ slits

NOTE: Size of each piece will depend upon desired size of finished bag.

Fold each piece in half as shown and sew a ½″ seam 9″ up from the fold on each side (Figure 1). Fold back the unsewn seam allowance ½″ and baste it down (Figure 2).

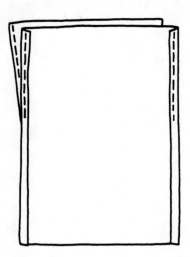

Figure 1

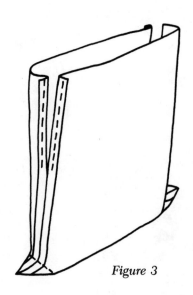

Figure 2

Figure 3

Lining

Figure 4

Press the seams open. At each of the lower points fold back the seam so that it falls directly on top of the bottom fold of the piece. Stitch a 2″ seam, as shown in Figure 3, at each of the points. Cut away the point, leaving a ¼″ edge beyond the seam. (NOTE: This will make the bag three-dimensional, rather than completely flat. This step can be omitted if desired). Turn the lining piece to the right side and slip it over the outside piece, aligning the seams. Pin and sew together the side openings of the lining and the outside bag (Figure 4).

Fold back and baste a ¼″ seam on each top edge (Figure 5). Push each edge through the slit of the handle, folding it over for one and one-half inch. Hem to the lining (Figure 6).

If you have difficulty obtaining wooden bag handles, make your own handles out of two 12″ long dowels, ⅜″ in diameter. Glue and insert each end into a large-holed bead. Hem the edges of the bag over the dowels. Then sew a ribbon, fabric, or braided rope handle over each dowel, attaching each end alongside a bead (Figure 7).

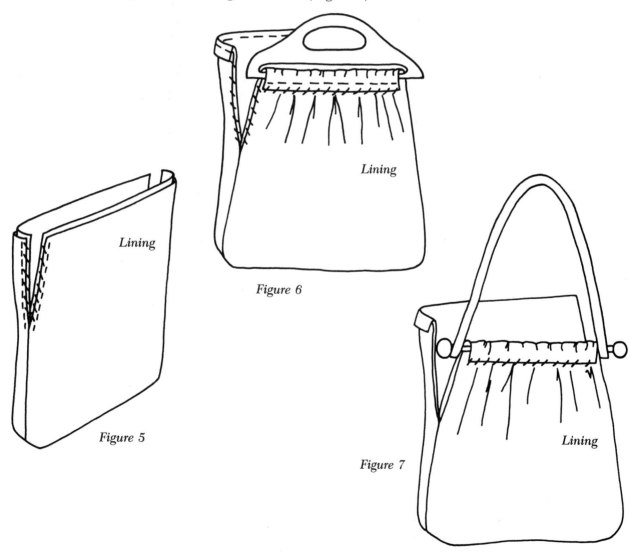

Lining

Figure 6

Lining

Figure 5

Lining

Figure 7

Decorated Store-Bought Bag

AN EVEN EASIER way to create an original bag is to add handcrafted decorations to one that you have purchased. There are many plain fabric bags being sold that could look quite distinctive with a bit of added trimming. Canvas bags and totes, especially, are made of pliable fabric and are easy to work on. Usually in a solid color, with contrasting color binding all around, they are plain enough to accomodate various kinds of decorations.

A bargello appliqué, done in colors to coordinate with the bag, is one possibility. Using any of the bargello patterns described in chapter 1, stitch an area that will fit the bag's flap (Figure 1), side, or handle. Hem back the raw edges of canvas and hem the piece to the bag. Full instructions for bargello appliqué are given in chapter 3, page 126. (See also color plate 7.)

A personalized canvas bag is an unusual gift. Following the needlepoint alphabet graph in chapter 6, stitch a name or a set of initials. Complete the stitched piece like the bargello appliqué and sew it to the bag.

Appliquéing pieces of fabric to the bag in a pattern is an even less involved process. An attractive appliqué for the flap would be the floral motif of the pot holder in chapter 3, appliquéd either in the "turned-edge" or the "iron-on" method. Other easy appliqué ideas are the large crocheted flower, stem, and leaves of the wall hanging in chapter 5; or the simpler, smaller crocheted flower used for the brimmed hat in this chapter.

If the bag you plan to trim is not lined with vinyl and the fabric can be stitched through easily, you could consider decorating it with embroidery. Any of the stitchery designs in chapter 5—the floral bouquet or one of the mini-stitcheries—can be embroidered directly on the bag. A few mirrors, stitched on a flap or along the shoulder strap, would also be charming accents.

With a little imagination you can adapt many other designs and ideas appearing throughout the book into novel decorations for store-bought bags, totes, and suitcases.

Figure 1

Belts

BELTS AND SASHES that are distinctive in design and coloration can add sparkle to simple dresses and coordinates. Making these useful accessories yourself enables you to fashion them in the colors, or combination of colors, that will best complement your clothes. As craft projects they are fun to do and uncomplicated in construction.

Macrame, with its interesting texture, makes ideal wrap-and-tie sashes. Different knot patterns for sashes are suggested here. Two are adapted from the necklace and choker designs, so you can even make a sash with matching jewelry for a coordinated fashion look. Any type of knotting cord can be used, from rugged-looking jute twine to more sophisticated, lustrous rayon rattail.

The bargello belt features a simple pattern which you begin stitching at the center back of the belt, working each side to the required length. A two-piece buckle is attached to the stitched piece to form a colorful and stylish belt. For a different look, stitch the bargello pattern 3″ or 4″ wide and sew strings to each end of the strip to make a front-tying, adjustable cinch belt. Besides making the belt in a variety of color combinations, consider adapting for belts any of the other bargello patterns described in chapter 1.

How to Make the Macrame Belt

MATERIALS:

any of the following knotting cords, in amounts
specified for each style belt:

        rug yarn
        jute twine
        rattail
        butcher twine
        cable cord

knotting board and pins
1½″ – diameter metal ring (Style One Belt)

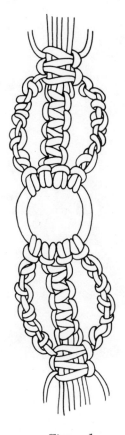

Figure 1

Style One

This type of belt requires a metal ring. This ring will fall at center back of the waist when the belt is worn. Either of two macrame patterns can be used—Wall Hanging Stripes *One* or *Three* in chapter 5. Cut each strand 5 yards long. Mount the number of strands necessary for the pattern onto the metal ring. Work the pattern for about 12″, leaving the rest unworked. Using a 24″ strand, make a wrapped knot around all the strands below the 12″ of pattern. Then mount the same number of strands on the other side of the ring, and work the other half of the belt the same way as the first (Figure 1).

Style Two

Two patterns—the Beaded Choker and the Multicolor Necklace in this chapter—can be adapted for belts. For each pattern, cut the strands 5 yards long. Work the pattern as specified in the instructions for these pieces, making 12″ of knotting on one side of the center, then 12″ on the other side. Tie all the strands together with wrapped knots, just as for the *Style One* belt, or trim the end of each strand with a bead.

How to Make the Bargello Belt

(As shown in color plate 7)

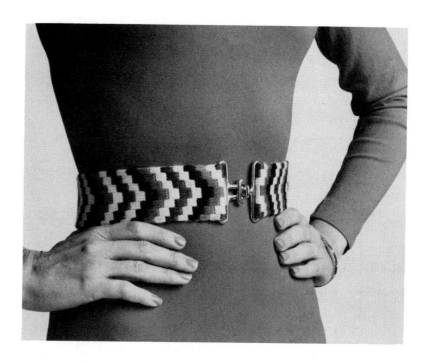

MATERIALS:

10-mesh mono, duo, or interlock canvas, a piece 4″ x 30″, or waistline measurement plus 4 inches

a harmonious combination of 4 or 5 colors, 1 ounce of each, in either worsted-weight yarn or 3-strand Persian-type yarn

a 2-piece belt buckle, similar to the one shown in Figure 1

1 yard of matching color grosgrain ribbon, ¼″ narrower than width of belt

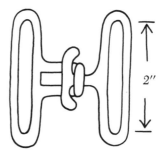

2″

Figure 1

Measure the buckle to determine the exact required width of the belt. Fold the strip of canvas in half and mark its center; this will be the center back of the belt. Holding the strip lengthwise, bring the needle up 10 meshes above the center back line and 2″ from the left edge of the strip. Following Figure 2, work the pattern to measure half the required belt width, adding or subtracting 3-stitch groupings as required. (*Note:* The stitch drawing represents the number of groupings necessary for a 2″-wide belt, and it ends with a 2-stitch grouping at either side.) Starting to the right of the first stitch made, work the right side of Row 1 (Figure 2).

Turn the piece around and work Row 1 on the other side of the center back line, thus forming a diamond. Using two other colors, fill in the center of the diamond (Figure 3). Depending on the width of the belt, there will be either more or fewer stitches made into the center of the diamond.

Figure 2

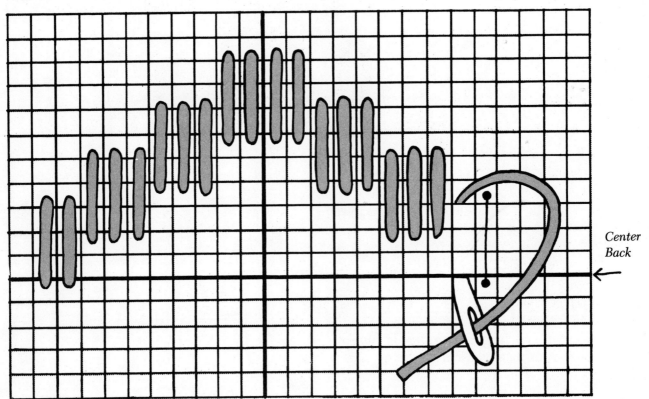

Center
Back

Figure 3

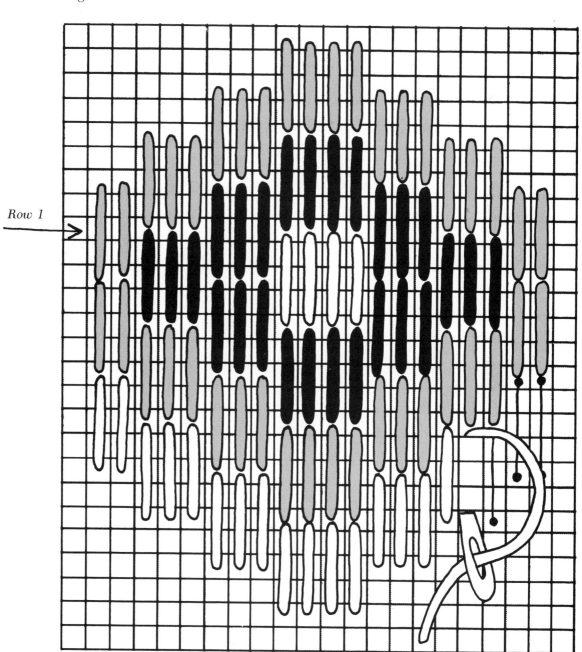

Row 1

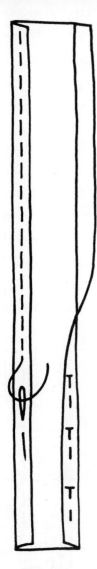

Continue working in rows on either side of the diamond, each row in a different color. (On a 2″-wide belt, a 24″ length of yarn is sufficient for making a row.) The completed belt strip should measure, on each side of the center back, one half the waistline measurement plus 2 inches.

To construct the belt, fold back the unworked edge on each side of the strip and baste it down without stitching through to the right side (Figure 4).

Draw one end of the strip through the slot in the buckle. Fold back and pin to the wrong side of strip. Repeat with other end of strip through other half of buckle. Try the belt on and adjust it to fit, making sure the center back diamond is positioned correctly. Cut away the unworked canvas and sew down each end (Figure 5).

Pin grosgrain ribbon to the back of the belt. Cut off excess length and fold back a ½″ hem on the cut end. Sew the grosgrain to the edge of the belt all around with small stitches (Figure 6).

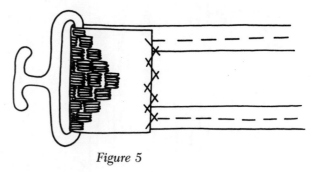

Figure 5

Figure 4

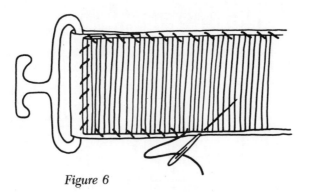

Figure 6

Jewelry

ANOTHER GREAT WAY to display your ability and accomplishment in a craft is to wear jewelry that you have created yourself. The handcrafted jewelry projects offered here are small scale, relatively simple projects. If you are a novice, completing a choker or a necklace almost effortlessly will give you the impetus and confidence to continue and become further involved in the craft. From a fashion point of view, handmade ornaments are important as smart, stylish accessories. Original and unusual handmade jewelry is worn with tailored daytime outfits, casual rugged sportswear, and sophisticated evening wear.

Any of the following pieces can be "made tonight, worn tomorrow." You will need a minimum of materials to create any of them: some string and beads for the macrame choker and necklace; some plastic rings, yarn, and possibly beads, for the crocheted ornaments. Very small amounts of these basic materials are required. Economical and simple to make, these pieces can be produced in multiples to serve as welcome gifts and bazaar items.

Necklace Made of Plastic Rings and Crochet

MATERIALS:

a package of plastic rings, ¾″ or 1″ diameter (8 in a package is standard for ¾″ rings)

1 ounce of yarn in any of the following materials:

> metallic yarn
> worsted yarn
> sport yarn
> crochet cotton, fine or medium weight

appropriate size hook for yarn being used (see chart in chapter 1)

Optional: beads

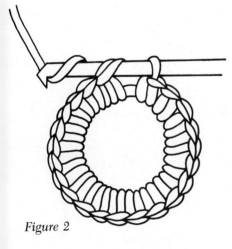

Figure 1

Crocheting over a Ring

Attach the yarn to the ring, as shown in chapter 1 (see Figures 32 and 33). Chain 1, then work single crochet stitches into the ring, crocheting around the edge (Figure 1). The object is to cover the ring completely with tightly worked stitches. It is not necessary to make a specific number of single stitches into each ring.

Once the ring is completely covered with stitches, join the beginning of the round to the end of the round by working a slip stitch into the first single crochet stitch made (Figure 2).

Figure 2

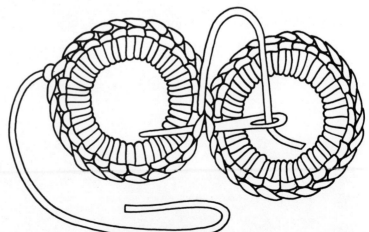

Figure 3

Fasten off the yarn, leaving a 10″ end. Use this end to sew adjacent rings together on the wrong side. After attaching them with a few overcast stitches (Figure 3), weave the needle through the back of the stitches a few times to secure the yarn. Then clip off the remaining length of yarn.

Making a 6-Ring Necklace

Make 6 crochet-covered rings. Arrange and join them as in Figure 4.

Attach the yarn in top right corner and chain a length to measure 16″. Slip stitch in the second chain from the hook and then in every chain up to the ring. Fasten off and weave the two ends through the back of the work. Make another tie-string on the other side of the pendant.

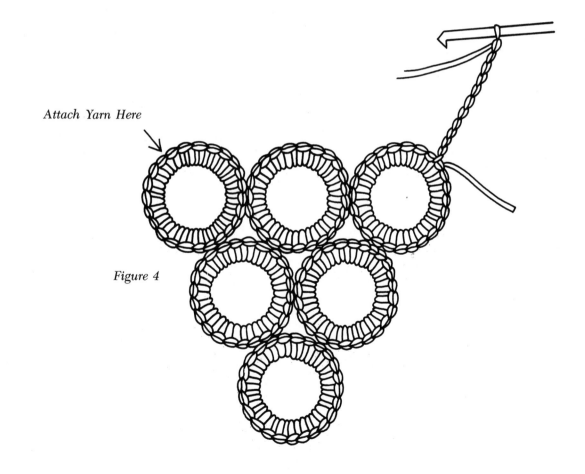

Attach Yarn Here

Figure 4

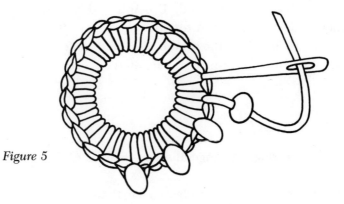

Figure 5

Beaded Variations

It is also possible to embellish a crocheted ring necklace with beads. Use round beads proportionate in size to the rings, small enough so that a few can be accomodated on each ring. To make any of the beaded necklaces shown, first construct the basic ring and tie-string structure. Then thread a fine needle with a length of the yarn used for crocheting, or a matching color sewing thread. Secure it to the ring by sewing through the back of a few stitches. Come up at the edge of the ring. Slip a bead on the needle, pulling it down to the ring. Insert the needle back into the edge, a stitch or two away. Come up again, two stitches away, and repeat the procedure (Figure 5). Distribute the beads around the rings as desired, or follow the layouts shown (Figures 6, 7, 8, 9).

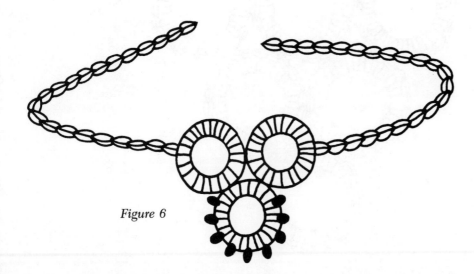

Figure 6

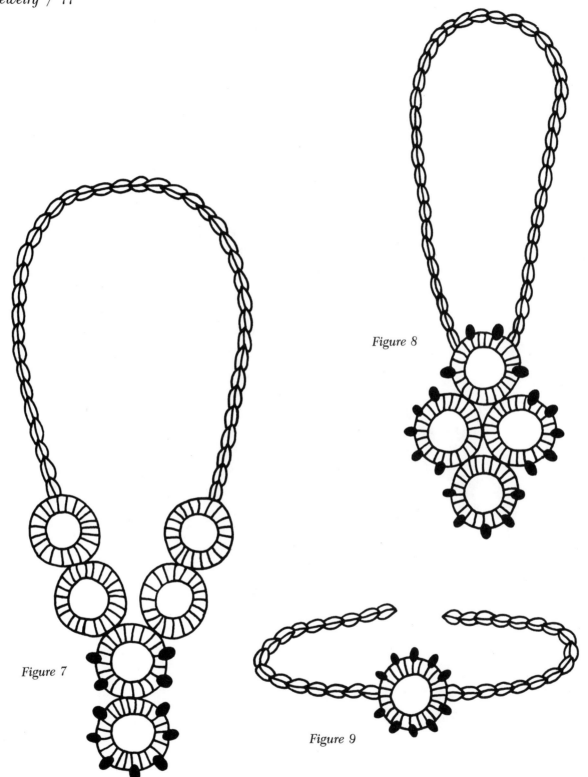

Figure 7

Figure 8

Figure 9

Beaded Macrame Choker

MATERIALS:
> 12 yards of any of the following:
>> jute twine
>>
>> rattail
>>
>> butcher twine
>>
>> medium-weight crochet cotton
>
> knotting board and pins
>
> 6 oval or 12 round beads, with holes large
> enough to pull through one strand of the
> knotting cord

Cut the 12-yard length into six 2-yard strands. Fold each in half and, pinning to the board at this middle point, place the strands alongside each other on the knotting board. Make 2 square knots on each 3-strand section (knotting with cords A & C, and D & F). Then

make a square knot with the anchor cords (B & E) over the two strands at center (cords C & D). Again, make 2 square knots on each section. Slip 1 oval bead, or 2 round beads one after the other, onto each anchor cord. Make 2 square knots on each section after the beads, then a square knot over the two center strands using the two anchor cords (Figure 1). Then, using the outermost strands A & F, make 3 square knots over all the other four strands (Figure 2).

Turn the work around and slip beads onto the anchor cords. This will be the center front of the choker. Then work the same knotting pattern on this side of the center front.

Try the choker around your neck. If the knotting does not go around to reach the center back, make more square knots on either side with strands A & F over all the other strands. Sometimes 7 or 8 knots are required rather than 3. On each side, tie the two center strands together to form the tie-string for the choker, as shown in Figure 2. The four other strands are trimmed to within ½″ from the last knot, and either sewn or glued to the back of the knotting. Make sure the strands are securely fastened and the ends do not show on the right side.

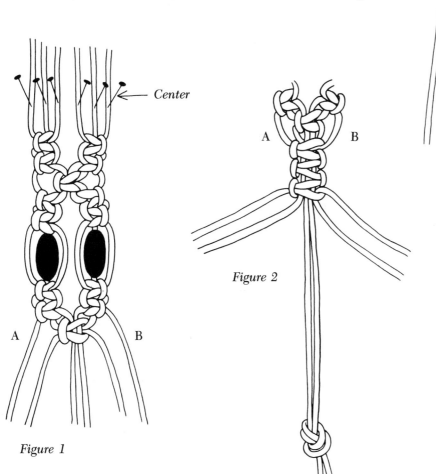

Center

Figure 3

Figure 1

Figure 2

Multicolor Macrame Necklace

MATERIALS:

    3 colors of knotting cord, two 3-yard lengths in
    each color, in any of the following:

- rattail
- jute twine
- rug yarn
- butcher twine
- medium-weight crochet cotton

    12 beads in a matching color
    knotting board and pins

Knotting the Strip

Pin the six lengths alongside each other on the board, 8″ from the
cut ends, arranging them as follows: 2 lengths Color A (A and B), 2
lengths Color B (C and D), 2 lengths Color C (E and F). Insert a pin

into A, as shown in Figure 1, and make an overhand knot 7″ away from the pin. Pin the knot to the board, diagonally stretching the strand across the others. Working from left to right, with B, make a double half hitch knot around A, then continue knotting around A with each of the other strands.

Untie the knot on A. Pin, knot and stretch B diagonally across, below A, and make double half hitch knots around it with the other strands. Stretch C across and knot around it.

Do not loosen the knot on C, but stretch that strand diagonally across the other strands from right to left. Make double half hitch knots around it with the other strands, working from right to left. Make two more diagonal double half hitch rows from right to left, completing a full 6-row repeat. A distinct pattern will be formed by the three colors.

Make 9 more 6-row repeats.

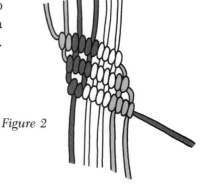

Figure 2

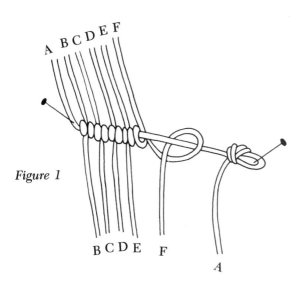

Figure 1

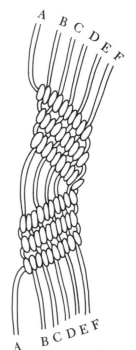

Figure 3

Forming the Necklace

Arrange the first and last repeats together side by side, making sure the rest of the strip is not being twisted. On the wrong side of the work, sew the two repeats together where they meet, using sewing thread. By the joining of the two, a diamond design will form in the center. Trim all the ends to one even length, 6″ below the knotting. String a bead onto each strand and knot the end to secure the bead.

Figure 4

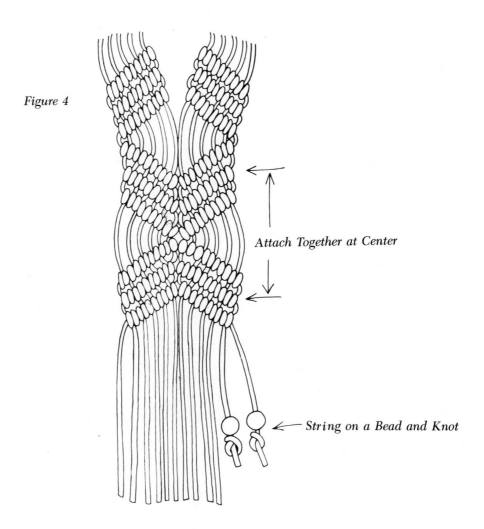

Attach Together at Center

String on a Bead and Knot

Shawls

CROCHETED SHAWLS ARE perennial favorites. Every woman, from teen-ager to grandmother, can find a use for a crocheted shawl to wear with anything from a casual calico dirndl skirt and peasant blouse to a formal, décolleté evening gown.

A shawl is not a "make-in-one-evening" project, but it is an easy accessory to crochet. Once you get started and establish the stitch pattern, you can continue working to completion without having to refer back to the instructions.

The two patterns featured here both produce triangular shawls, but each achieves the triangular shape differently. The easier of the two, the mesh pattern shawl, is worked from the longest side and decreased on each side until a triangle is formed. The other shawl, made up of clusters of three triple crochet stitches, begins as a small triangle and grows into a large triangular shawl. This pattern can be crocheted in a multicolor stripe effect. The mesh pattern shawl cannot be striped, but for color interest, try crocheting it in a variegated yarn containing many colors. This multicolor yarn will create an attractive and unpredictable pattern.

Both these designs can be used to make shawls suitable for both day and night. All the popular knitting yarns, from fine crochet cotton, metallics, and bouclés, to the heavier worsted, and rug yarns, can be fashioned into useful, appealing shawls.

Crocheted Mesh Shawl

MATERIALS:

12 ounces of yarn in any of the following materials:

> worsted yarn
> sport yarn
> rug yarn
> fine or medium-weight crochet cotton
> metallic yarn, crepe, bouclé, mohair, or other novelty yarn

appropriate size hook for yarn being used (see chart in chapter 1)

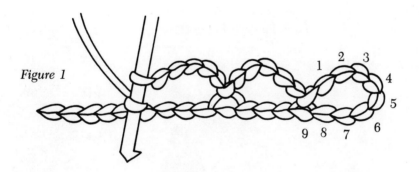

Figure 1

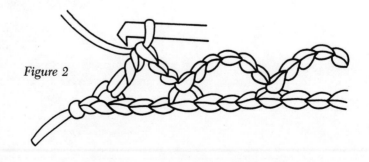

Figure 2

Crocheting the Mesh Pattern

Make a length of chain stitches that measures 66″ long.

Row 1: Sl st in ninth ch from hook, *ch 5, skip 3 chs, sl st in next ch (Figure 1); repeat from * across till there are about 4 chs left from the knot. Ch 2, skip 3 chs, dc in next ch. Ch 5, turn (Figure 2).

Note: There will no doubt be extra chains not worked into after the last stitch of this row is made. Later, when the shawl is done, open the knot at the end of the chains. Undo the extra chains one by one. Thread the end of this yarn into a large-eyed needle and weave it through the back of the stitches. Clip it close to the work.

Row 2: Sl st in next mesh, *ch 5, sl st in next mesh; repeat from * across, without working into the last mesh. Ch 2, dc in last mesh. Ch 5, turn (Figure 3).

Repeat Row 2 for pattern, decreasing two meshes on each row until there is only one mesh left at the point of the shawl (Figure 4). Fasten off. Weave the end through the back of the work.

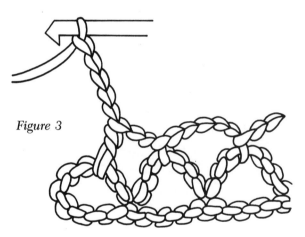

Figure 3

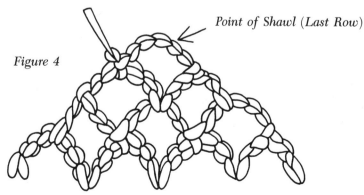

Figure 4

Point of Shawl (Last Row)

Fringing

Each of the meshes on both short sides of the shawl is trimmed with a fringe (Figure 5). Following directions in chapter 1 cut the yarn into 12″ strands. For each fringe, use five strands folded in half.

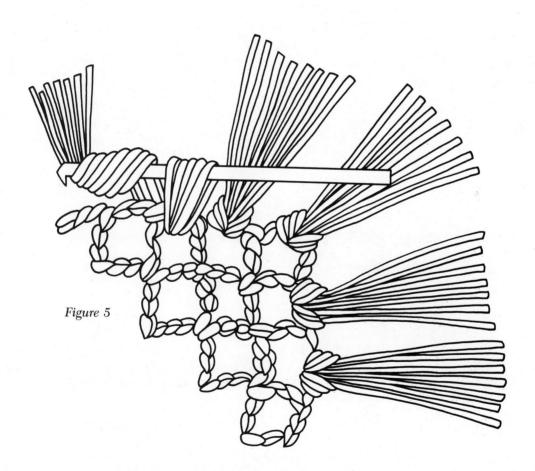

Figure 5

Crocheted Cluster Stitch Shawl

MATERIALS:

14 ounces of any yarn listed for mesh shawl
appropriate size hook

Stitch pattern

Row 1: Ch 4, sl st in first ch in form ring, ch 6, into the ring work 3 trc, ch 4, 3 trc, ch 2, 1 trc. Ch 6, turn (Figure 1).

Row 2: 3 trc into first sp, ch 2, (3 trc, ch 4, 3 trc) in center ch-4 sp, ch 2, (3 trc, ch 2, 1 trc) in last sp. Ch 6, turn (Figure 2).

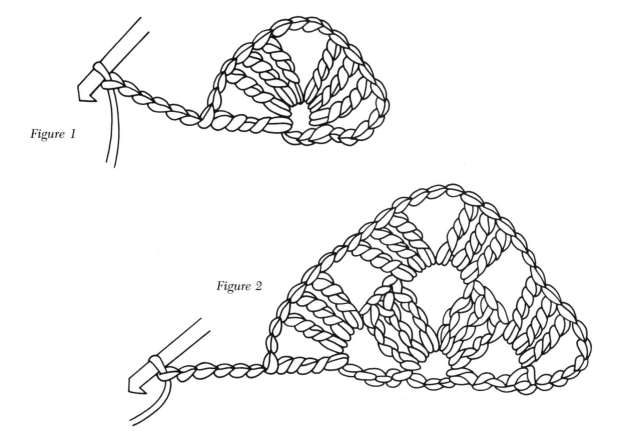

Figure 1

Figure 2

Row 3: 3 trc in first sp, ch 2, 3 trc in next sp, ch 2, (3 trc, ch 4, 3 trc) in ch-4 sp, ch 2, 3 trc in next sp, ch 2, (3 trc, ch 2, 1 trc) in last sp. Ch 6, turn.

Row 4: 3 trc in first sp, (ch 2, 3 trc) in each sp till corner ch-4 sp, (3 trc, ch 4, 3 trc) in ch-4 sp, (ch 2, 3 trc) in each sp till last sp, (3 trc, ch 2, 1 trc) in last sp. Ch 6, turn.

Repeat Row 4 and work until shawl measures 60″ across the longest of the three sides. Fasten off and weave the ends through the back of the work.

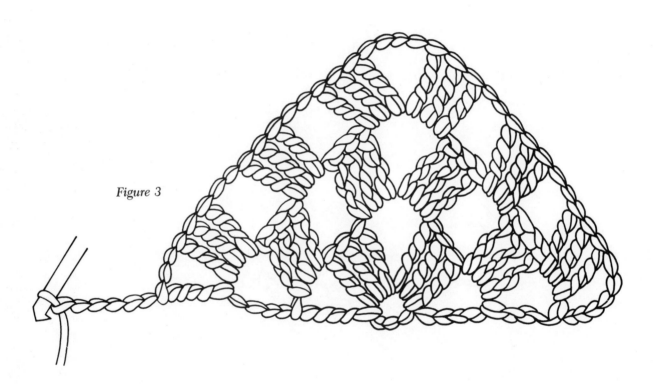

Figure 3

Making a Striped Shawl

In combining yarns of different colors and textures, make sure they are of similar weight so all your stitches will be the same size. To change colors for a striped effect, complete the last stitch of the row. Instead of chaining 6 at the end of the row with the same color, chain 6 in a new color. Cut the first color yarn, leaving a 3″ end. Proceed, making the next row with the new color.

Fringing

Each ch-2 space on the two short sides of the shawl, and the ch-4 space at the point, is trimmed with a fringe. Following directions for fringing in chapter 1, cut the yarn into 12″ strands. For each fringe, use 5 strands folded in half.

Decorating Store-Bought Clothes

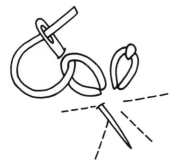

Lazy Daisy Stitch

THE NUMEROUS DESIGNS and craft techniques introduced in this book can be imaginatively adapted to give simple store-bought or home-sewn clothes a handcrafted look. All sorts of garments can be trimmed with crafts—T-shirts, man-tailored shirts, sweaters, skirts, dresses, and jeans, as well as children's and infants' wear. This type of project is ideal as a single evening's undertaking since most clothes require a mere accent to transform them into unusual, one-of-a-kind pieces.

Any of the miniature embroidery motifs in chapter 5 can be stitched on yokes of blouses, fronts of T-shirts, and jeans. The greeting card floral border can be stitched as a frame around an embroidered name, or set of initials, creating a personalized T-shirt or sweater. The technique of mirror embroidery can be used for decorating necklines, cuffs, and collars on simple man-tailored shirts or formal evening

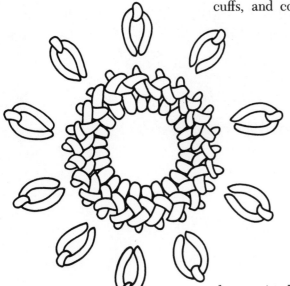

Mirror Embroidery

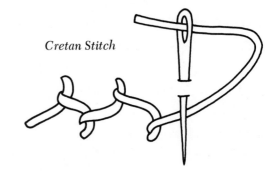

Cretan Stitch

dresses. Appliqués done in different crafts, such as the crocheted floral appliqués in this chapter and in chapter 5, and the fabric floral appliqué for the pot holder in chapter 3, can also be sewn to the back of a blouse or the hem of a skirt. Crocheted rings or macrame strips can be sewn around necklines, thus creating garments with jewelry attached.

With a little imagination and a few materials, you will find these mini-projects challenging and lots of fun to do.

Crocheted Hats

CROCHETED HATS ARE very easy accessories to make. Beginners, especially, will be delighted by how quickly they can see a finished product. Depending on how proficient you become in the craft, a simple hat like the openwork cloche can be completed in as little as one hour.

The three hats featured are simple, classic shapes. Though hat styles vary from year to year, the cloche and the brimmed hat are universally popular. Any type of yarn can be used to make these three hats, but when you crochet with your choice of yarn, using the specified size hook, the gauge must match the one given. If the yarn is too fine, crochet with two or three strands together in order to match the gauge.

You might consider making a brimmed hat for the winter using several strands of mohair, and then making the same hat in straw for the summer. Both versions of the openwork hat would be striking done in metallic yarn for evening, and lovely in worsted yarn for day. These hats are so easy to make that you can produce a whole wardrobe of hats, one in every color, to match your every outfit.

Openwork Cloche Hat

MATERIALS:

2 ounces of worsted yarn, or any other yarn or
combination of yarns that will result in the
specified gauge
Size H or I crochet hook

GAUGE: 4 dc stitches = 1″

SIZE OF HAT: Instructions are given for *Small Size* (Head size
18″–20″) and *Medium Size* (Head size 22″–24″).

Round 1: Ch 4, sl st in first ch to form ring, ch 4, (dc in ring, ch 1) seven
times. Sl st in third ch of ch-4 (Figure 1). (*NOTE:* Join all the following
rounds the same way.) (8 spaces around.)

Round 2: Sl st into ch-1 sp, ch 4, dc in same sp, ch 1, (dc, ch 1) twice in
each of the next 7 spaces (Figure 2). Join. (16 spaces around.)

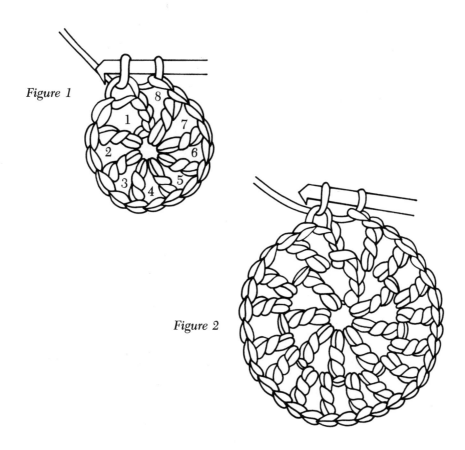

Figure 1

Figure 2

Round 3: Sl st into ch-1 sp, ch 4, dc in same sp, ch 1, *dc in next sp, ch 1, (dc, ch 1) twice in next sp; repeat from * around (Figure 3). Join. (24 spaces around.)

Round 4: Sl st into ch-1 sp, ch 4, dc in same sp, ch 1, *(dc, ch 1) in each of next 2 spaces, (dc, ch 1) twice in third space; repeat from * around (Figure 4). Join. (32 spaces around.)

Round 5: Sl st into ch-1 sp, ch 4, dc in same sp, ch 1, *(dc, ch 1) in each of next 7 spaces for *Small Size* (Figure 5A), or 3 spaces for *Medium Size* (Figure 5B), (dc, ch 1) twice in next sp; repeat from * around. Join.

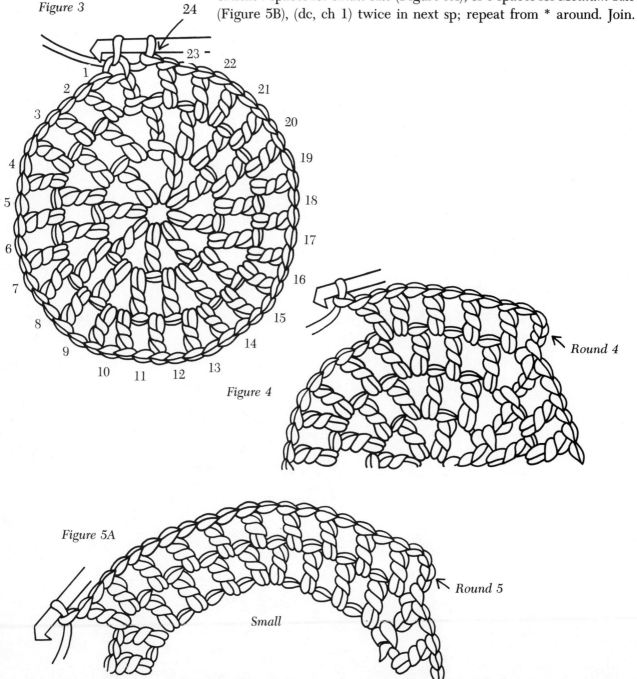

Figure 3

Figure 4

Round 4

Figure 5A

Round 5

Small

Round 4

Round 6: Sl st into ch-1 sp, ch 4, *dc in next sp, ch 1; repeat from * around (Figure 6). Join. Repeat Round 6 till piece measures 7″ from top of crown.

Edging

Work a single crochet stitch into every dc and every ch-1 space around (Figure 7). At the end of the round, sl st into the first sc made. Make two more single crochet rounds. Fasten off the yarn and weave the ends through the back of the stitches.

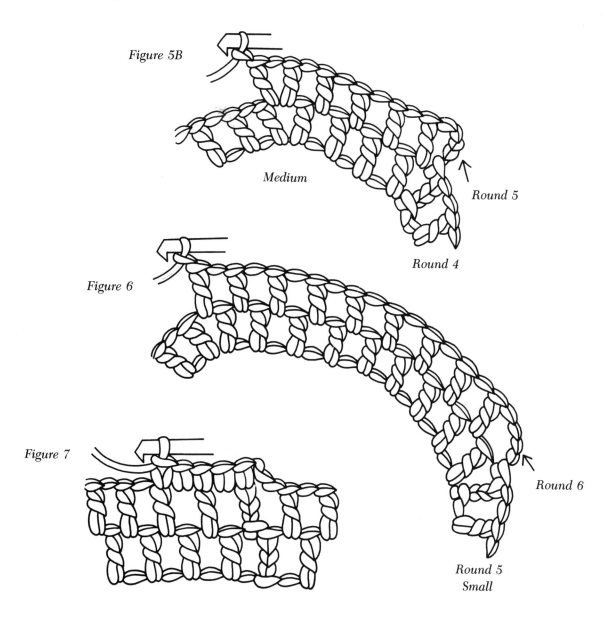

Figure 5B

Medium

Round 5

Round 4

Figure 6

Figure 7

Round 6

Round 5
Small

Openwork Hat with Lacy Brim

MATERIALS:

2 ounces of worsted yarn or any other yarn or combination of yarns that will result in the specified gauge; 1 ounce of yarn in a contrasting color, or ½ ounce each in 2 contrasting colors.

Size H or I crochet hook

GAUGE: 4 dc stitches = 1″

SIZE OF HAT: Instructions are given for *Small Size* (head size 18″–20″) and *Medium Size* (head size 22″–24″).

Color Plate 1

CENTER: 36″ by 48″ baby quilt, made from 12 appliquéd squares; pattern in chapter 3, instructions in chapter 5.

TOP: Matching knife-edge pillow with pre-gathered eyelet lacing sewn around the edges; pillow instructions in chapter 3, pattern in chapter 3.

BOTTOM RIGHT: Wooden-handled crazy-quilt bag; instructions in chapter 2, crazy quilt instructions in chapter 1.

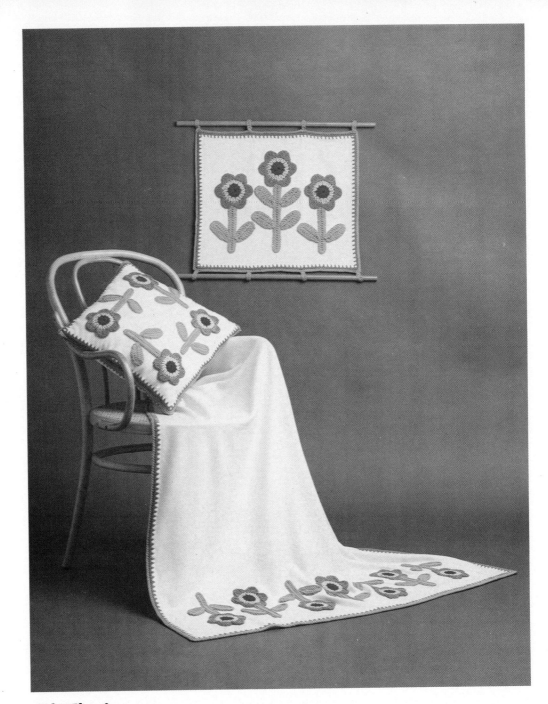

Color Plate 2
TOP: Wall-hanging with crocheted appliqués, chapter 5.
CENTER: 18″ by 18″ knife-edge pillow, chapter 3.
BOTTOM: Afghan with crocheted appliqués, chapter 3.

Color Plate 3

UPPER RIGHT: Bargello appliqué nailed to fabric-covered wood, stitch pattern and color guide in chapter 3, basic bargello wall hanging instructions in chapter 5.

CENTER: Wine bottle covered with worsted-weight yarn, chapter 3.

LOWER RIGHT: Appliquéd flower pot, chapter 4.

LOWER LEFT: Pillow appliquéd with bargello diamond motifs, chapter 3.

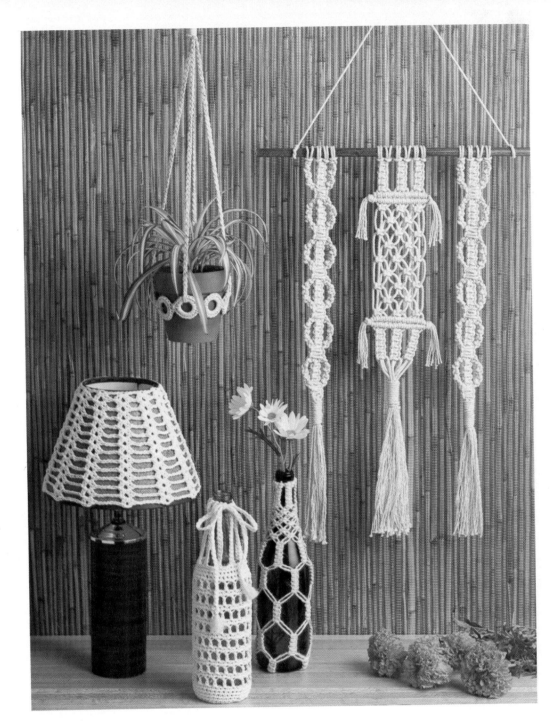

Color Plate 4
UPPER LEFT: Crocheted rings hanging planter, chapter 4.
UPPER RIGHT: Macrame hanging, with strips one and two, chapter 5.
BOTTOM CENTER: Macramed and crocheted wine bottle covers, chapter 3.
LOWER LEFT: Crocheted lampshade, chapter 3.

Figure 1

← *Lace Braid Through this Row*

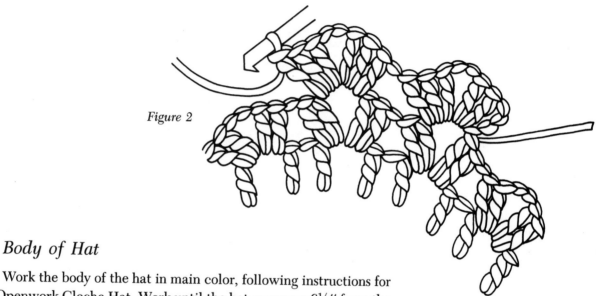

Figure 2

Body of Hat

Work the body of the hat in main color, following instructions for the Openwork Cloche Hat. Work until the hat measures 6½″ from the top of the crown. Fasten off main color. Do not work the single crochet rounds.

Brim

Round 1: Attach contrasting color A in any ch-1 sp, (ch 3, dc, ch 2, 2 dc) in same sp, *ch 1, skip one ch-1 sp, in next ch-1 sp work (2 dc, ch 2, 2 dc), (Figure 1); repeat from * around. Ch 1, sl st in third ch of ch-3. Fasten off color A.

Round 2: Attach contrasting color B in any ch-2 sp, (ch 3, 2 dc, ch 2, 3 dc) in same sp, *ch 1, (3 dc, ch 2, 3 dc) in next ch-2 sp (Figure 2); repeat from * around. Ch 1, sl st in third ch of ch-3. Fasten off color B.

Figure 3

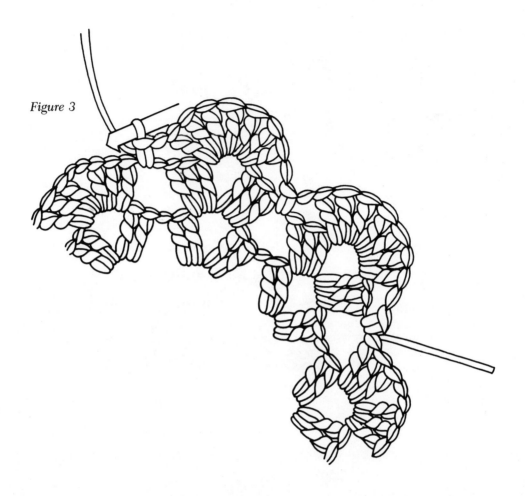

Round 3: Attach the main color or contrasting color A in any ch-1 sp, sc in same sp, *ch 1, work 7 dc in next ch-2 sp, ch 1, sc in next ch-1 sp; repeat from * around (Figure 3). Sl st in first sc made. Fasten off.

Weave all the ends through the back of the stitches.

Optional Tie

Cut six 42″-strands of any of the colors. Knot all 6 strands together at one end. Braid them, using 2 strands in each braiding section. Knot the end of the braid. Weave the braid through the holes which make the bottom row of the body of the hat, as shown in Figure 1. Try the hat on, adjust the tie to fit, and tie both ends into a decorative knot.

Bulky Brimmed Hat with Flower Appliqué Trim

MATERIALS:

    8 ounces of yarn in any of the following materials:

> rug yarn
>
> 2 strands of worsted yarn (totaling 8 ounces)
>
> 3 strands of sport yarn (totaling 8 ounces)

    scraps of worsted yarn in 3 colors for the flower appliqué

    Size I or J crochet hook

GAUGE: 3 sc stitches = 1″   3 sc rows = 1″

SIZE OF HAT: One size fits 18″, 20″, and 22″ head.

Figure 1

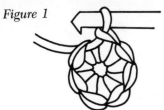

Figure 2

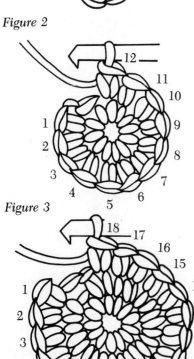

Figure 3

Crown of Hat

Round 1: Ch 2, work 6 sc stitches in second ch from hook, sl st into first sc made. Ch 1.

Round 2: Work 2 sc stitches in joining st and in each of next 5 sts. Sl st in first sc made. Ch 1. (12 sc stitches around.)

Round 3: 2 sc in joining st, *sc in next st, 2 sc in next st; repeat from * around. Sl st in first sc made. Ch 1. (18 sc around.)

Round 4: Repeat Round 3. (27 sc stitches around.)

Round 5: Sc in joining st and in each st around. Sl st into first sc made. Ch. 1.

Round 6: 2 sc in joining st, *sc in each of next 2 sts, 2 sc in next st; repeat from * around. Sl st into first sc made. Ch 1. (36 sc around.)

Round 7: Repeat Round 5.

Round 8: 2 sc in joining st, *sc in each of next 3 sts, 2 sc in next st; repeat from * around. Sl st into first sc made. Ch 1. (45 sc around.)

Round 9: Repeat Round 5.

Round 10: 2 sc in joining st, *sc in each of next 4 sts, 2 sc in next st; repeat from * around. Sl st into first sc made. Ch 1. (54 sc around.)

Round 11: Repeat Round 5.

Round 12: 2 sc in joining st, *sc in each of next 8 sts, 2 sc in next st; repeat from * around. Sl st into first sc made. Ch 1. (60 sc around.)

Repeat Round 5 for 12 more rounds, or until crown measures 7″ from the very top. Join with a sl st at the end of each round.

Figure 4

7″

3″

Work
into
front
loop
of
stitch

Figure 6

Back Loop

Front Loop

Figure 5

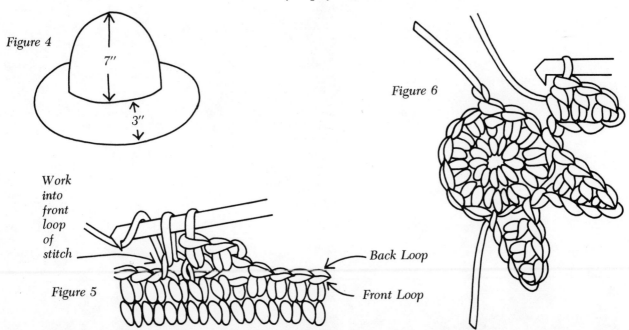

Brim

Round 1: Ch 1, *working into the front loops of last round's stitches,* (Figure 5), sc in joining st and in next 4 sts, *2 sc in next st, sc in next 5 sts; repeat from * around. Sl st in first sc made. Ch 1. (70 sc around.)

Round 2: Sc in joining st and in every st around. Sl st in first sc made. Ch 1.

Round 3: 2 sc in joining st, * sc in next 6 sts, 2 sc in next st; repeat from * around. Sl st in first sc made. Ch 1. (80 sc around.)

Round 4: Repeat Round 2.

Round 5: 2 sc in joining st, *sc in next 7 sts, 2 sc in next st; repeat from * around. Sl st in first sc made. Ch 1. (90 sc around.)

Round 6: Repeat Round 2.

Round 7: 2 sc in joining st, *sc in each of next 8 sts, 2 sc in next st; repeat from * around. Sl st in first sc made. Ch 1. (100 sc around.)

Round 8: Repeat Round 2.

Round 9: 2 sc in joining st, *sc in each of next 9 sts, 2 sc in next st; repeat from * around. Sl st in first sc made. Ch 1. (110 sc around.)

Round 10: Repeat Round 2. Fasten off.

Attach yarn on inside of hat in *back loop* of any sc st of last round of *crown*. Ch 1, sc in same st and then sc *tightly* in back loop of every st around. Sl st in first sc made. Fasten off. Steam-press brim lightly to flatten it.

Flower Appliqué

(See also appliqué pillow, color plate 5)

Round 1: In Color A ch 4, sl st in first ch to form ring, ch 1, work 8 sc into ring. Sl st in first sc made. Fasten off.

Round 2: Attach Color B in any sc, ch 1, work 2 sc in same st, then work 2 sc in each of the remaining 7 sc sts around. Sl st in first sc made. Fasten off. (16 sc around.)

Round 3: Attach Color C in any sc, *ch 4, sc in second ch from hook, hdc in each of next 2 chs, sl st into next 2 sc sts on ring (Figure 6); repeat from * around, making eight petals. Sl st in st where yarn was attached. Fasten off. Weave all ends through back of stitches. Using sewing thread, sew the appliqué to the inside brim of the hat, so that when the hat is worn, the appliqué will show on the up-turned brim.

Decorative Home Accessories

3

One way to decorate your home distinctively is to fill it with unusual handmade accessories. This chapter features a variety of small, unique items that can highlight any room of your house. A collection of colorful pot holders can be hung in the kitchen, handcrafted placemats can be arranged on a dining room table, and empty wine bottles— covered with crochet or macrame—can be placed on shelves or on small end tables in the living room.

Shown in this chapter, too, are ways you can redecorate with a minimum of expense. An old or faded lampshade can be covered with an unusual crocheted covering. Simple, inexpensive fabric pillows can be trimmed with bargello, fabric, or crocheted appliqués.

If you enjoy using and decorating with afghans, you will be pleased to find an afghan design that is, like the other projects in this chapter, quick and easy to make.

106

Pot Holders and Placemats

BECAUSE THEY ARE so small, pot holders are about the easiest home accessories to make. As craft projects they are ideal for beginners. Since they can be made—and very quickly too—in a variety of craft techniques, they give beginners an opportunity to learn and practice a new craft while creating a useful kitchen accessory.

Pot holders are made from two squares of fabric which have a piece of batting or terry cloth sandwiched between them. This layer of stuffing serves as insulation, protecting hands when picking up hot pots and pans. Both sides of the pot holder can be decorated with either fabric appliqués, crocheted appliqués, or embroidery. Or each side can be constructed from fabric pieces in a crazy-quilt pattern of different prints.

Placemats (and fabric doilies for placing under vases) do not require the layer of batting, but they are decorated and constructed the same way as pot holders. While usually made in 9″ x 13″ rectangles, they can also be made in round or oval shapes of any size. A decorative purchased fringe or other trimming can make them look even more attractive when the trimming is sewn all around, or simply on both ends of the mat (Figures 1 and 2).

Since pot holders and placemats will undergo a great deal of use and will often get soiled, it is important to make them of washable fabrics. Cottons and cotton blends are ideal. If you plan to trim these items with embroidery, make sure the threads you use are colorfast.

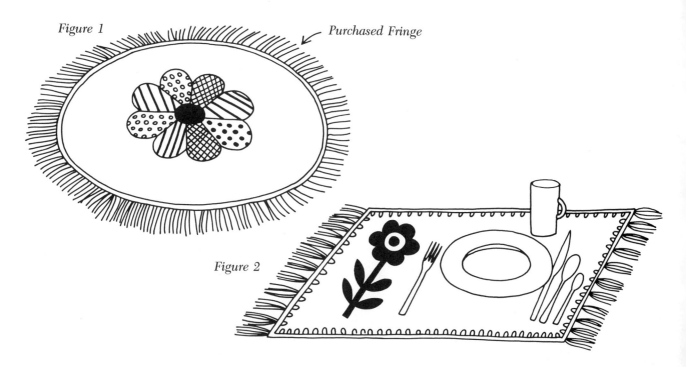

Figure 1

Purchased Fringe

Figure 2

Appliquéd and Quilted Pot Holder

MATERIALS:

    scraps of cotton fabric, preferably calicoes,
      ginghams
    two pieces of matching color solid cotton
      12″ x 12″
    one piece of cotton batting or terry cloth
      12″ x 12″
    plastic ring, crochet cotton, and appropriate
      size hook

Note: Instructions for attaching the appliqué in the turned-edge technique are given below. If you wish, you can apply it by the iron-on method explained in chapter 1.

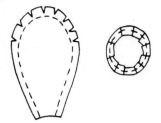

Figure 1

Make templates for the petal and center patterns, and cut 8 petals and 1 center (Figure 1). For best results in achieving a patchwork look, cut each petal from a different print, and the center from a solid color fabric. Clip around the upper edges of the petals and center (Figure 2).

Attach every 2 adjacent petals together, sewing a 2½″ long seam. Press the seams open (Figure 2).

Pin back the clipped upper edge of the petals ¼″ and baste it down. Do the same with the center (Figure 3).

Hem the 8-petal piece to the center of the 12″ x 12″ square. Then attach the flower center, covering the raw edges of the petal (Figure 4). If desired, make an appliqué on the other square.

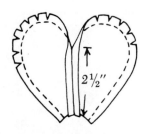

Figure 2

Place the two squares together, right sides facing. Cover one side with the batting or terry cloth. Sew a ½″ seam all around, leaving 3″ unsewn on one side (Figure 5). Trim the seam to ¼″. Turn the piece to the right side through the opening. Push out all four corners to make them neat and angular. Sew up opening. Working through all three layers, do a few rows of stitching, by hand or by machine, around the motif and along the edge of the square.

Following instructions given for the Crocheted Rings Jewelry in chapter 2, make a crocheted ring and attach it to one corner of the pot holder.

(For other uses of this motif see quilt and pillow, color plate 1.)

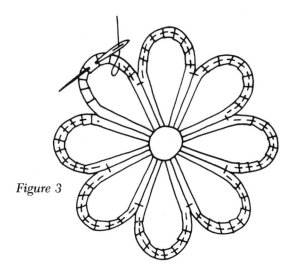

Figure 3

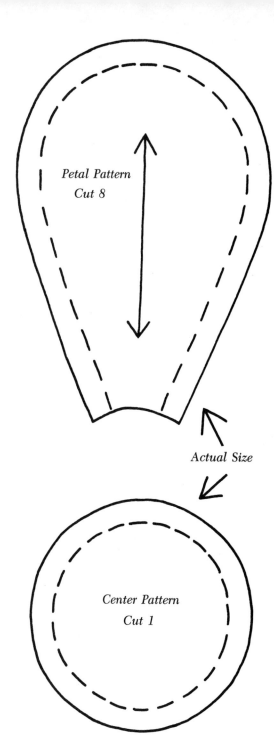

Petal Pattern
Cut 8

Actual Size

Center Pattern
Cut 1

Figure 4

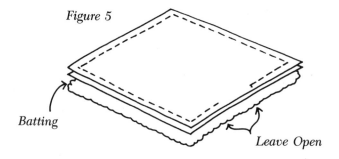

Figure 5

Batting

Leave Open

Decorating Bottles

WINE AND OTHER beverages are often packaged in graceful, imaginatively shaped glass containers. You can transform these attractive empty bottles into flower vases, lamp bases, and decorative accessories to highlight shelves and tables in your home.

Once you have removed labels by soaking the bottle in hot water, you have a smooth, clean surface which you can decorate in any number of exciting ways. You can brush diluted white glue onto the bottle and then permanently attach pieces of fabric to it in a crazy-quilt pattern. The method for applying the fabric and later glazing the bottle is the same as that used for making the appliquéd planter in chapter 4.

Various colors of yarn, straw, or rope can also be glued to the bottle, starting from the top and working downwards, encircling the bottle to cover it fully, as shown in color plate 3. A glaze can later be applied to the yarn-covered bottle to make a shiny, spongeable surface.

A crocheted cover is very quickly and easily made, especially the one featured. This one is done in an open-mesh pattern. It is first crocheted, and is then pulled on and tied to the bottle. This can serve as a clever gift to take along to a dinner party, along with the bottle of wine. Since the crocheted cover can be untied and taken off, the hostess can later remove the bottle's label.

The macramed cover, which takes a little more time to make, is constructed directly on the bottle and is fitted to the bottle's shape. Almost any shape or size bottle can be covered in this manner, provided proper allowances are made in the length of the strands. Variations of this design could include the insertion of beads between the knots, using different knots, or knotting various colors together to form multicolor patterns.

Crocheted Bottle Cover

(As shown in color plate 4)

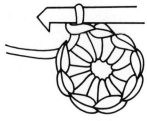

Figure 1

MATERIALS:
    2 ounces of any of the following yarns:
        raffia or synthetic straw
        worsted yarn
        sport yarn
        fine or medium-weight crochet
          cotton
    appropriate size hook for yarn being used (see
      chart, chapter 1)

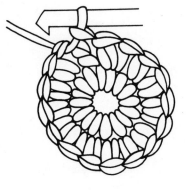

Figure 2

This cover is designed for a straight wine bottle of any length.

Base of Bottle

Round 1: Ch 4, sl st in first ch to form ring, ch 1, work 8 sc into ring. Sl st in first sc made (Figure 1).

Round 2: Ch 1, 2 sc in joining st, 2 sc in each of next 7 sc. Sl st in first sc made (Figure 2). (16 sc around.)

Make as many of the following rounds as are necessary to cover the base of the bottle:

Round 3: Ch 1, 2 sc in joining st, sc in next st, *2 sc in next st, sc in next st; repeat from * 6 times. Sl st in first sc made. (24 sc around.)

Round 4: Ch 1, 2 sc in joining st, sc in each of next 2 sc, *2 sc in next st, sc in each of next 2 sts; repeat from * 6 times. Sl st in first sc. (32 sc around.)

Round 5: Ch 1, 2 sc in joining st, sc in each of next 3 sts, *2 sc in next st, sc in each of next 3 sts; repeat from * 6 times. Sl st in first sc. (40 sc around.)

Figure 3

Round 6: Ch 1, 2 sc in joining st, sc in each of next 4 sts, *2 sc in next st, sc in each of next 4 sts; repeat from * 6 times. Sl st in first sc. (48 sc around.)

Round 7: Ch 1, 2 sc in joining st, sc in each of next 5 sts, *2 sc in next st, sc in each of next 5 sts; repeat from * 6 times. Sl st in first sc. (56 sc around.)

Continue in this fashion until crocheted circle fully covers base of bottle (Figure 3).

Then work the following rounds:

Round 1: Ch 1, sc in joining st, sc in each st around. Sl st in first sc made. Repeat this round until there is a ¾″ lip extending up from the crocheted circle (Figure 4).

Body of Bottle

(Openwork pattern)

Round 1: Ch 4, *skip 1 st, dc in next st, ch 1; repeat from * all around (Figure 5). Sl st in third ch of ch-4 (Figure 6).

Round 2: Ch 1, sc in joining st, sc in next sp, *sc in next dc, sc in ch-1 sp; repeat from * around (Figure 7). Sl st in first sc made.

Repeat Rounds 1 and 2 of the openwork pattern until a long tube is formed which covers the tubular part of the bottle, except for ¾″ at the top. Try the cover on the bottle to check the fit. Then work a few

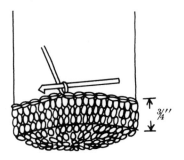

Figure 4

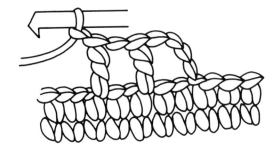

Figure 5

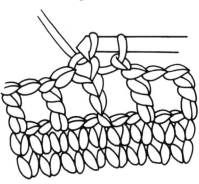

Figure 6

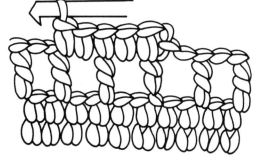

Figure 7

single crochet rounds to form a ³⁄₄″ border at the top of the pattern. Do not fasten off the yarn.

Neck of Bottle

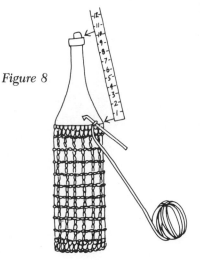

Figure 8

While cover is on the bottle, measure from top of the border to the top of the bottle (Figure 8). Take cover off and make a row of chains for the length required. Skip 7 chains, sl st in next ch and every chain across (Figure 9). Sl st in next 3 sts on the last row of the border. Chain the same number of chains as before and make another string with a hole at the top. Crochet these strings all around the border. Fasten off the yarn and weave the end through the back of the stitches.

Following Figure 10 cut 6 strands of yarn 30″ long. Braid them together, with a knot and fringe at either end. Lace the braid through the holes at the top of the strings. Pull cover onto the bottle and tie the braid into a decorative knot.

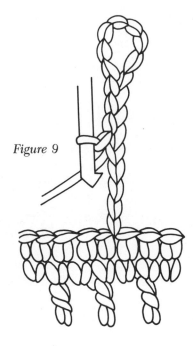

Figure 9

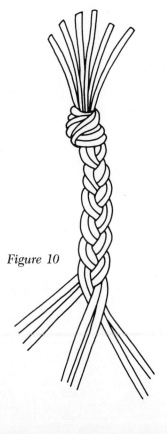

Figure 10

Macrame Bottle Cover

(As shown in color plate 4)

MATERIALS:

 32 yards of any of the following materials:
    butcher twine
    rug yarn
    jute twine
    rattail yarn
    cable cord
 knotting board and pins

Note: Length specifications are given for making a cover for a 12-inch long and 3-inch diameter bottle. To cover a fatter and taller bottle, cut each strand about one yard longer.

Cut the 32 yards into the following lengths: two 1-yard lengths and ten 3-yard lengths.

Holding the two short strands together, fold them in half and pin their centers to the board. Make an overhand knot 4″ from the center on each side. Pin the knots to the board to form a holding cord. Fold each long strand in half and mount its center to the holding cord with a lark's head knot. On each group of 4 strands make 5 square knots, one after the other and worked tightly (Figure 1).

Unpin the holding cord and undo the overhand knots. Wrap the holding cord around the top of the bottle, and tie it tightly and securely (Figure 2).

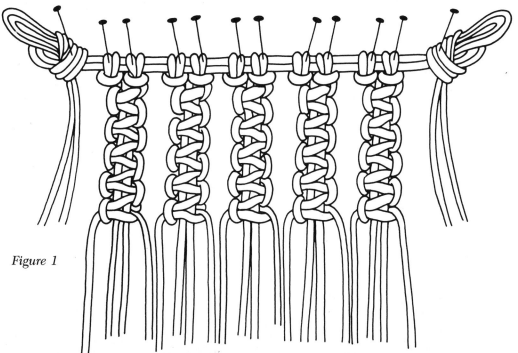

Figure 1

Insert all four ends of the holding cord into the bottle to keep them out of the way.

Neck of Bottle

Place the bottle at the edge of a table, so that the strands fall over the edge of the table. Working in an alternate square knot pattern, make one round of these knots, turning the bottle around as each knot is completed. Then make 5 more rounds of alternating square knots, spacing the knots on each round to conform to the increasing thickness of the bottle (Figure 3). At the end of the six rounds, the knotted section should be so secure that it does not slip down.

Body of Bottle

*Make one more round of alternating square knots, then follow with 4 more square knots on each section (5 knots made on each section). Repeat this pattern, from *, forming diamond shapes which conform to the shape of the bottle, until the base is reached. The last grouping of 5 square knots should extend beyond the lower rim of the bottle. Turn the bottle upside down, holding it steady, and continue to work on the base. If the five knotted sections do not meet at the center of the base, make more knots. Thread a needle with a double strand of sewing thread and sew the five sections securely together at the center of the base, at the same time pulling the cover so it fits snugly (Figure 4). Cut away excess lengths, and apply white glue to the cut ends. Overlap them and flatten the surface. Allow the glue to dry.

Take the four holding cords out of the bottle. On each group of 2 strands, tie a 5-inch length of alternating double half hitch knots (Figure 5). Tie an overhand knot over all four ends. Cut away excess lengths, leaving a 1″ fringe.

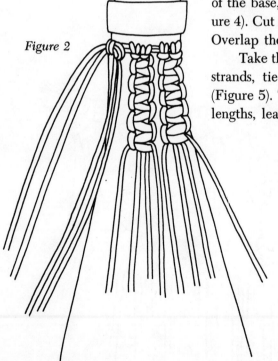

Figure 2

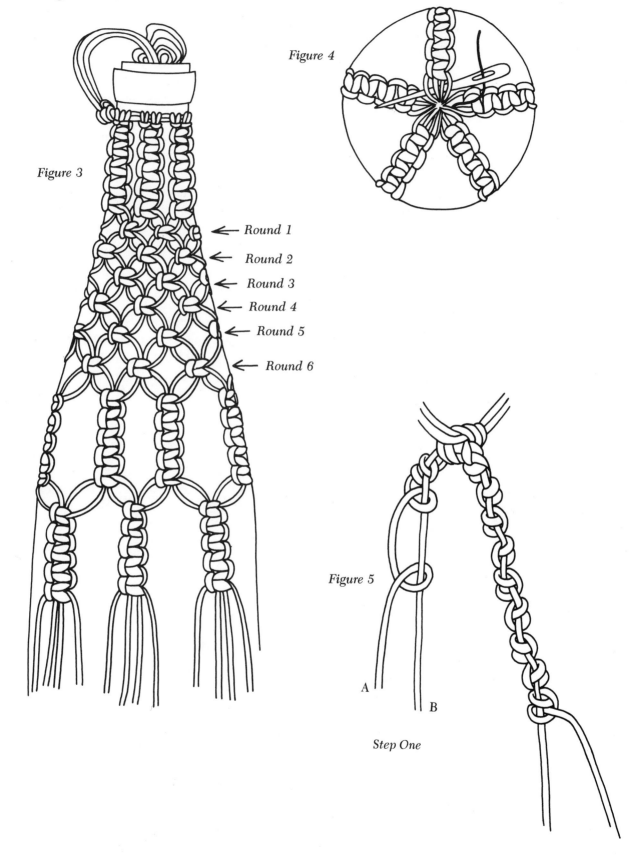

Figure 3

Figure 4

← *Round 1*

← *Round 2*

← *Round 3*

← *Round 4*

← *Round 5*

← *Round 6*

Figure 5

A

B

Step One

Lampshades

LAMPS ARE IMPORTANT accessories in any home. They serve not only to illuminate the room, but to brighten and accent it with their styling.

Simple hanging and table lamps can easily be transformed into exciting decorative accessories by handcrafting them in any number of ways. Fabric shades can be trimmed with fabric appliqués, crocheted appliqués (Figure 1), or strips of bargello (Figure 2). Rather than sewing the appliqués to the shade, you can place the shade over the arm of an ironing board and attach the appliqué to it with the *iron-on* technique explained in chapter 1. A vinyl shade can be decorated by glueing fabric appliqués to it, using the same technique as for making the appliquéd planter in chapter 4.

Cone-shaped paper and fabric shades can be covered with an attractive open-work crochet bonnet. This crocheted covering can be made in a variety of materials to fit the mood of the room's decor, ranging from natural fibers—like jute—to colorful worsted yarn. Another approach worth considering is to stripe the covering simply by changing colors on every round. Not only will you create a very distinctive, unusual lamp, but you will be able to use yarns left over from other projects.

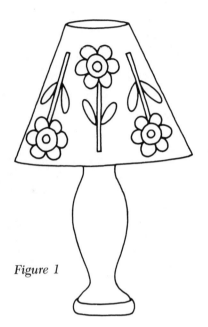

Figure 1

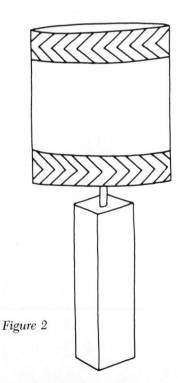

Figure 2

Crocheted Lampshade Cover

(As shown in color plate 4)

THIS LAMPSHADE COVER is designed for a cone-shaped fabric or paper shade, attached to a metal frame, whose top opening is narrower than the opening at the bottom.

MATERIALS:

    4 ounces of any of the following yarns:

        worsted yarn

        rug yarn

        sport yarn

        metallic yarn

        crepe yarn

        fine or medium-weight crochet

          cotton

    appropriate size hook for yarn being used (see chart, chapter 1)

Make a length of chains to fit loosely around the top opening of the shade. Count the number of chains made. If the figure is not divisible by 5, add or subtract the appropriate number of chains. Being careful not to twist the row of chains, sl st into the first chain made, to form a large ring.

Round 1: (ch 3, dc, ch 2, 2 dc) into the joining ch, *ch 1, skip 4 chs, (2 dc, ch 2, 2 dc) into next ch (shell made); repeat from * around. At the end of the round ch 1, sl st into the third ch of ch-3 at beginning of the first shell. *Note:* Depending on the yarn used, there will be either more or fewer shells than the number appearing in Figure 1.

Figure 1

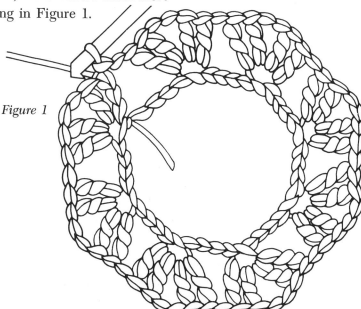

Round 2: Sl st into next dc and into ch-2 sp, (ch 3, dc, ch 2, 2 dc) in same sp, *ch 2, (2 dc, ch 2, 2 dc) in ch-2 sp of next shell; repeat from * around (Figure 2). Ch 2, sl st in third ch of ch-3 of first shell made.

Round 3: Sl st into next dc and into ch-2 sp, (ch 3, dc, ch 2, 2 dc) in same sp, *ch 3, (2 dc, ch 2, 2 dc) in ch-2 sp of next shell; repeat from * around. Ch 3, sl st in third ch of ch-3.

As shown in Figure 3, the pattern involves making one more chain between the shells on each successive round. However, the pattern may sometimes have to be adjusted to make a properly fitting cover. The crocheted piece must be tried on the shade after each round is completed. If the last completed round fits rather loosely around the shade, work the next one or two rounds with the same number of chains separating the shells as on the last completed round. If it fits snugly, make an extra chain between the shells on the next round.

When the crocheted piece fully covers the shade, fasten off the yarn and weave the ends into the back of the stitches. Place the cover on the shade, adjusting the rows of shells so they form straight, vertical rows. Using a double strand of sewing thread, sew the chains at the top and bottom of the crocheted piece to the shade.

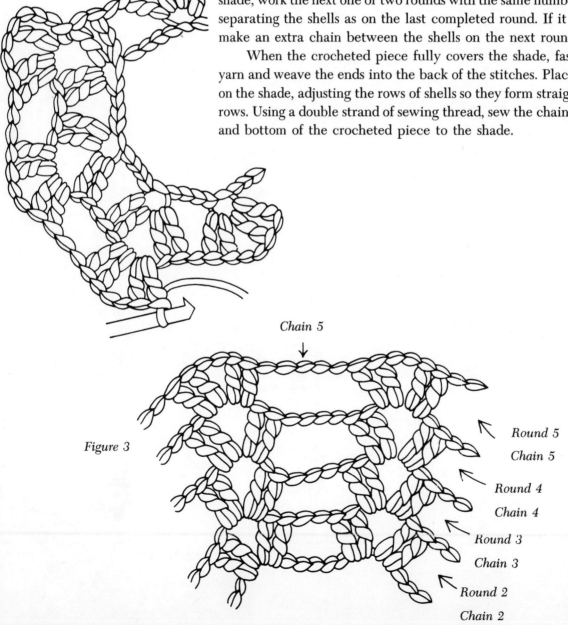

Figure 2

Figure 3

Chain 5

Round 5
Chain 5

Round 4
Chain 4

Round 3
Chain 3

Round 2
Chain 2

Afghans

USUALLY MEASURING 4 feet in width and 5 feet in length, a crocheted or knitted afghan is not a one-night or a one-week project. Those lacking the time or the patience to create these practical accessories in the traditional manner, will delight in this new and simple technique for making afghans.

Warmth, the essential feature of all afghans, can be derived from a 48″ x 60″ piece of softly textured, solid color woolen fabric, such as flannel. The fabric is trimmed with crocheted floral appliqués—either the small flowers appearing in the hat pattern in chapter 2, which can be sewn to the fabric in an allover pattern, or the large flowers featured in the wall hanging design in chapter 5, which can be arranged in a border pattern on the short sides of the afghan. The fabric's raw edges are finished with a crocheted edging of single crochet around all four sides, as shown for the wall hanging, and then each short side is trimmed with a row of fringes attached to the single crochet stitches.

This technique is not only useful for making afghans of many sizes, including small baby afghans and carriage covers, but also bedspreads and throws for sofas. In the amount of time it ordinarily takes to make one afghan, you will be able to complete a collection of flower-trimmed coordinates. These can include an afghan, a pillow or two, and a wall hanging.

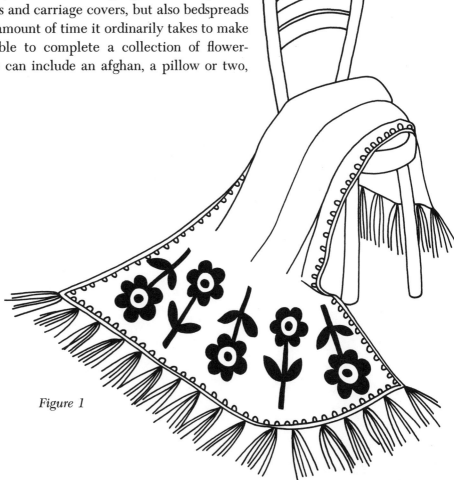

Figure 1

Flower-Trimmed Afghan

(As shown in color plate 2)

MATERIALS:

    $1\frac{1}{4}$ yards of 60″-wide white flannel

    worsted yarn in the following quantities and
      colors:

          8 ounces hot pink
          8 ounces green
          2 ounces cranberry
          2 ounces light pink

    aluminum crochet hook size H

    steel crochet hook size 2 for crocheting first
      round of edging

Following instruction for the crocheted appliqué in chapter 2, make 14 flowers, crocheting the rounds in the following colors:

Round 1: Cranberry
Round 2: Light pink
Round 3: Hot pink

Crochet 14 stems in green, and 28 leaves.

Cut away the selvages of the fabric. Arrange 7 flowers on each *short* side of the piece, as in the design shown in the color plate. Sew the appliqués down. Then crochet the edging (single crochet) all around, making Rounds 1 and 2 in hot pink and Round 3 in green. If you wish to fringe both short sides of the afghan, purchase an extra 4 ounces of yarn in the desired fringe color (Figure 1). Follow instructions for fringing in chapter 1.

Pillows

ONE WAY TO add verve and excitement to the decor of any living room, bedroom, or family room is to introduce a grouping of colorful, unusual pillows.

Pillows are easy accessories to make. Their constructions and shapes vary, the simplest type to make being the knife-edge pillow. This style consists of two squares of fabric that are sewn together to form a pocket into which stuffing is inserted. Plain knife-edge pillows can successfully accent a sofa or chair, especially when made from leftover fabric that was used for making a tablecloth or curtains, thus achieving a coordinated look. By devoting a little more time and effort

Clockwise from upper left: Pillow appliquéd with crocheted flowers of brimmed hat (chapter 2) and wall hanging (chapter 5). Pillow with bargello diamond appliqués (chapter 3). Pillow with crocheted flower appliqués and crocheted edging (chapter 5). Pillow with bargello appliqué (pattern shown in chapter 6), with purchased trim. Pillow with floral appliqué of pot holder flower (chapter 3), with pre-gathered eyelet lace trim. Crocheted plaid pillow. Segment of patchwork wall hanging pattern (chapter 5) made into a pillow.

to decorating the pillow, you can create more unusual, unique pieces. Consider, too, decorating ready-made plain fabric pillows using any of the following techniques.

Many designs featured in other projects in this book can be adapted for pillows simply by appliquéing the crafted piece to the pillow, before or after the pillow is made. These versatile designs include the floral bouquet embroidery in chapter 5, which can be stitched on a square of fabric, sewn to the pillow, and then trimmed around the raw edges with colorful ribbon (Figure 1); the floral appliqué of the pot holder in chapter 3 (Figure 2); the crocheted flower for the brimmed hat in chapter 2; and the large flower appliqué for the wall hanging in chapter 5. Using the knife-edge pillow's simple principle of two-piece construction, you can make any of these pillows in a rectangular or round shape. Another approach is to create the pillow from squares made entirely from small pieces of fabric sewn together. Choose from any of the patchwork patterns in chapter 5; or sew together appliquéd felt shapes that have crocheted borders all around. Make into square or rectangular pillows (Figure 3).

Following are three more novel ideas for decorating these useful accessories, each demanding little in the way of time and/or materials—two distinctive canvas-work patterns for making attractive bargello appliqués, and a clever method of creating a plaid effect in crochet.

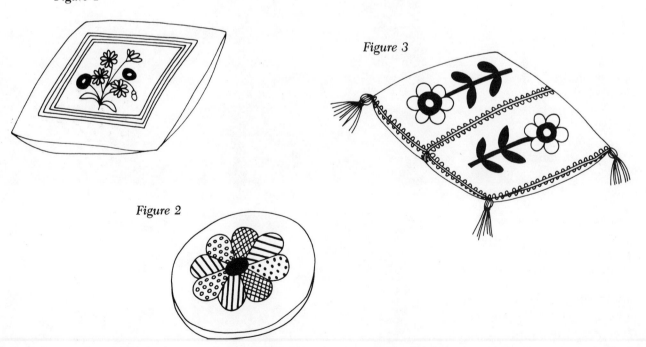

Figure 1

Figure 3

Figure 2

General Directions for Making the Knife-Edge Pillow

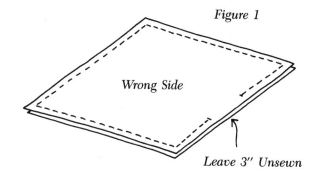

Figure 1

Wrong Side

Leave 3" Unsewn

MATERIALS:
$\frac{3}{4}$ yard of any of the following fabrics:
- felt
- corduroy
- velveteen
- hopsacking or linen

1 pound package of polyester, or cotton, pillow stuffing

Though the popular sizes for pillows are 14″ square and 16″ square, it is possible to make a knife-edge pillow in any size desired. Out of the $\frac{3}{4}$ yard of fabric cut two identical size squares, allowing $\frac{1}{2}$″ for a seam all around beyond the dimensions desired for the completed pillow. Place the squares one on top of the other, right sides facing. Sew a $\frac{1}{2}$″ seam all around, leaving a 3″ opening on one side (Figure 1). Trim off the point at each of the four corners to form neater, flatter corners when the pillow is turned (Figure 2). Turn the piece to the right side through the opening and push out each of the corners to form neat right angles (Figure 3). Insert stuffing through the opening, generously filling all four corners. Sew both sides of the opening together (Figure 4).

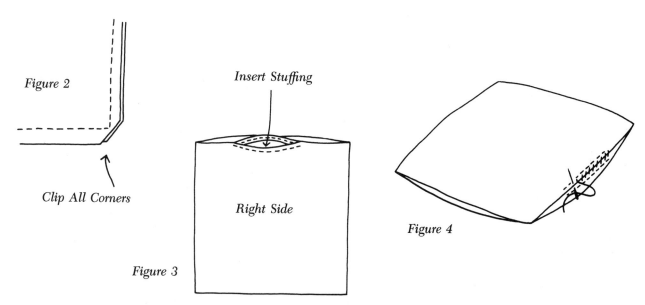

Figure 2

Clip All Corners

Insert Stuffing

Right Side

Figure 3

Figure 4

Diamond–Shaped Bargello Appliqué for Pillow

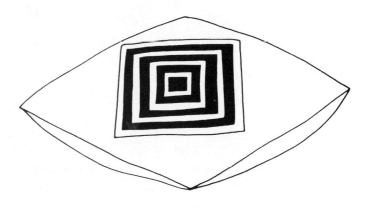

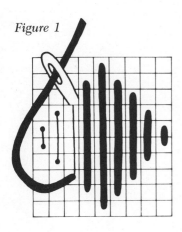

Figure 1

Figure 2

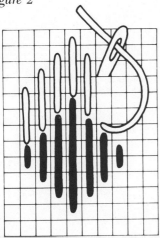

(As shown in color plate 3)

MATERIALS:
    10″ x 10″ piece of 10-mesh needlepoint canvas
    a selection of three of four colors, 1 ounce of
    each, in either of the following:
        worsted yarn
        Persian-type needlepoint yarn (3-
        strand)

Fold the piece of canvas in half in both directions to determine the center point. Following Figure 1, work the center diamond in any one of the colors. In another color, work the next round, stitching in sections as shown—top section (Figure 2), bottom section, and then the two sides (Figure 3) to complete the diamond shape. Stitch as many more rounds as desired, making each round in a different color.

126

When diamond measures desired size, work a backstitch in any color at the edge of the last round (Figure 4).

Trim the canvas so that a ½″ unworked edge remains all around. Clip the point of each corner to about ¼″ from the backstitch row. Fold the edge to the wrong side and baste it down, forming neat angular corners (Figure 5).

Center and pin the diamond to one side of a ready-made pillow, or one square of a pillow before it is constructed. Sew it down all around with small, imperceptible stitches, using a double strand of sewing thread (Figure 6).

Figure 4

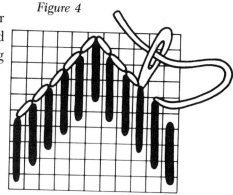

COLOR COMBINATION USED FOR THE APPLIQUÉS
ON PILLOW AND WALL HANGING APPEARING IN COLOR PLATE 3

Center Diamond—Cranberry. Round 4—Off-White
Round 1—Red   Round 5—Olive Green
Round 2—Orange   Round 6—Flag Blue
Round 3—Yellow   Round 7—Royal Blue

Figure 3

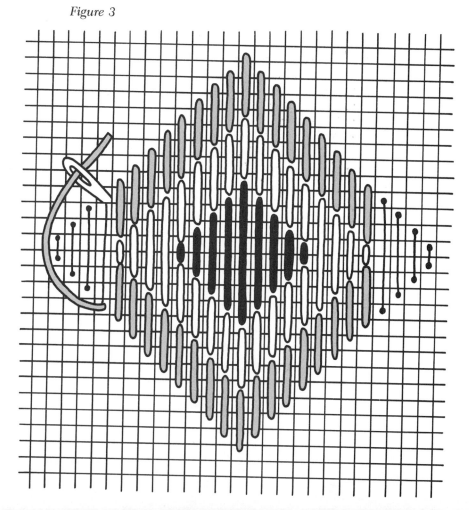

Figure 5

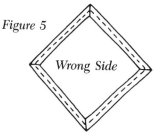

Wrong Side

Figure 6

Crocheted Plaid Pillow

(As shown in color plate 5)

COMPLETED PILLOW MEASURES 16″ x 16″.

MATERIALS:

4 ounces of worsted yarn in each of 3 colors
that contrast: one light color (A), one color
that is medium in value (B), and one color
that is very dark (C).

Some Possible Color Combinations

A—Beige	A—White	A—White
B—Rust	B—Red	B—Lilac
C—Brown	C—Navy	C—Purple

aluminum crochet hook size G or H, whichever
makes the specified gauge

¾ yard of fabric; stuffing for pillow

GAUGE: 2 meshes = $1\frac{1}{8}$″

Figure 1

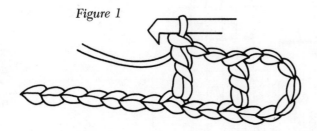

Figure 2

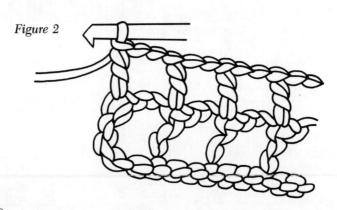

Color Plate 5

TOP: Patchwork wall decoration, made from calicos and white cotton, mounted and framed, chapter 5.

CENTER: Crocheted plaid pillow, chapter 3.

BOTTOM LEFT: 16″ diameter round pillow, appliquéd with crocheted flower of wall hanging in chapter 5, and crocheted flowers of brimmed hat in chapter 2.

BOTTOM RIGHT: Crocheted striped planter cover, chapter 4.

Color Plate 6

TOP: Bargello wall-hanging, chapter 5.

CENTER: Bargello planter, chapter 4; stitch pattern shown in chapter 3.

BOTTOM LEFT: Patchwork knife-edge pillow, made from a section of patchwork wall
decoration pattern in chapter 5; rust diamond in center is appliquéd.

BOTTOM RIGHT: Rectangular knife-edge pillow with bargello appliqué and purchased
edging sewn onto edges as trim; stitch pattern in chapter 6, knife-edge pillow
instructions in chapter 3.

Color Plate 7

CLOCKWISE FROM UPPER LEFT:

Pencil holder—soup can covered with bargello; stitch pattern in chapter 6, instructions in chapter 4 (bargello planter).

Telephone book cover; stitch pattern in chapter 1, instructions in chapter 6.

Bargello picture frame; chapter 6.

Bargello belt; chapter 2.

Bargello strip sewn to bottom of clutch bag's flap; stitch pattern shown in chapters 1 and 3, instructions in chapter 2.

Color Plate 8
TOP: Three miniature embroideries with fabric mat, chapter 5.
CENTER: Floral embroidery framed in an embroidery hoop, chapter 5.
BOTTOM LEFT: Greeting card with mirror-embroidered border, chapter 6.
BOTTOM RIGHT: Greeting card with floral border, chapter 6.

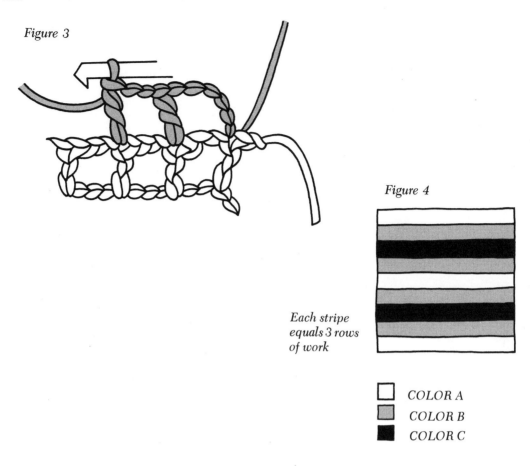

Figure 3

Figure 4

*Each stripe
equals 3 rows
of work*

☐ COLOR A
▨ COLOR B
■ COLOR C

Making the Mesh Background

With Color A, ch 86 loosely.

Row 1: Dc in eighth ch from hook, *skip 2 chs, ch 2, dc in next ch (Figure 1); repeat from * across. (27 holes made.) Ch 5, turn.

Row 2: Dc in second dc, *ch 2, dc in next dc; repeat from * across. After working in last dc, ch 2, skip 2 chs after the last dc made, dc in next ch (Figure 2). Ch 5, turn.

Row 3: Repeat Row 2. Fasten off Color A. Turn.

Row 4: Attach Color B in first dc, ch 5, *dc in next dc, ch 2; repeat from * across (Figure 3), working last dc of the row the same way as on Row 2. Ch 5, turn.

Work 2 more rows in Color B to complete the 3-row stripe. Then work a 3-row stripe in Color C. Continue crocheting the stripes in the order designated in Figure 4, completing 9 stripes and 27 rows of meshes.

Weaving

For best results, do the weaving with the mesh piece resting on a flat surface. Cut a 7-yard length of Color A. Fold it in half and thread the two ends together through a large-eyed tapestry needle. Adjust all four strands so they are even in length. Beginning in the first row of holes and working at right angles to the stripes, weave the four strands from one edge of the piece to the other, going over and under the bars separating the holes. Then weave the strand through the second row of holes in the opposite direction (Figure 5), and the third row in the same direction as the first row. Cut the strands, leaving a 5″ end extending from the edge of the piece. Working in the same manner, weave the next 3 rows in Color B. Following Figure 4 for color arrangement, and making 3 rows of weaving for each color, weave through all the holes of the mesh piece, thus forming a plaid pattern. If necessary, loosen or tighten some rows of weaving so that the plaid is square in shape. Do not weave all the ends through the back of the stitches. These will be hidden from view when the plaid piece is sewn to the pillow.

Edging

Attach Color C in any hole on any edge of the piece. Ch 1, sc in same sp, * ch 1, sc in next hole at the edge; repeat from * all around. Sl st to first sc made. Fasten off.

Making the Pillow

Measure the dimensions of the plaid square. Add ½″ seam allowance all around. Cut two pieces of fabric to these dimensions and make a knife-edge pillow. Lay the plaid piece on top of the pillow. Push all loose strands under the plaid piece. Pin it to the pillow all around, matching the corners. Using a double strand of sewing thread, sew the plaid piece to the pillow, working the stitches into the pillow's seam so that the piece completely covers one surface of the pillow (Figure 6).

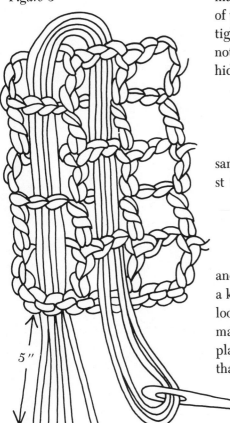

Figure 5

5″

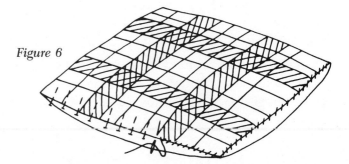

Figure 6

Bargello Appliqué
for Pillow

(As shown in color plate 6)

MATERIALS:

  10″ x 10″ piece of 10-mesh needlepoint canvas
  a selection of 3 or 4 colors, 1 ounce of each, in
    any of the following:
              worsted yarn
              Persian-type needlepoint yarn (3-
                strand)
  1 yard of purchased trim such as ribbon, knitted
    trim, metallic trim, etc. to sew around the
    appliqué

Make the appliqué in the bargello pattern featured here (Figure 1), or choose any of the patterns described in the other chapters.

Work an 8″ x 8″ square, in any of these patterns, within the 10″ x 10″ canvas piece, adjusting the length of the stitches at top and bottom of the bargello pattern accordingly so that a perfect 8″ square is formed. Trim away the excess canvas, leaving a ½″ unworked edge. Center the piece on the pillow and baste the edge down. Pin the purchased trim at the edge of the square, covering the unworked canvas completely. Miter the trimming at the corners, if it is wide; if

135

it is narrow and flexible, pin it around each of the points to form rounded corners. Join the two raw edges of the trimming where they meet. Then sew down the trimming, attaching one edge to the pillow, the other to the bargello square.

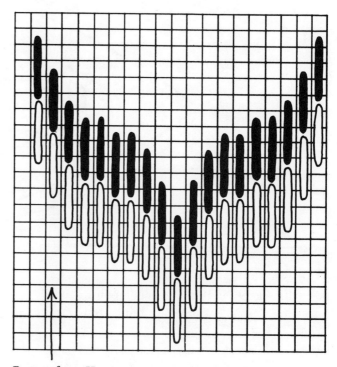

Repeat from Here

Some Other Ideas

This technique can also be used for making rectangular appliqués, or smaller individual square pieces to be scattered over a large pillow. Also, the various bargello patterns can be combined and imaginatively arranged on one canvas square to form exciting bargello patchwork patterns.

Planters and Pots —————————4

Healthy potted plants can bring a pleasant accent of greenery to your home, whatever its decorative style may be. You can arrange and display plants in a variety of ways—by placing them on windowsills, shelves, and tables; by suspending them from ceilings, near windows; or by hanging them from special decorative brackets attached to walls, room dividers, and window frames.

Pots of many shapes, sizes, and designs are available, since decorating with plants is a popular means of introducing vitality and excitement into homes. With a minimum of time and expense you can create a unique collection of plant accessories yourself. You can purchase rustic, inexpensive clay pots and decorate them with fabric appliqués, or dress these pots with colorful crocheted covers. You can recycle a large tin can and make it into a planter covered with a bargello sleeve that is coordinated with a pillow or wall hanging you've done in the same canvas-work pattern. For hanging clay, plastic, or ceramic pots, you can make stable, attractive holders in macrame or crochet.

As craft projects, all these items are easy to make, requiring only basic skills in each craft. The materials are few and are available in most hardware and craft stores. As gifts, these plant accessories are ideal. On any occasion when you may want to give someone a potted plant, consider giving the plant along with a hanging holder or cover that you have made yourself.

Hanging Planter Made of Crocheted Rings

(As shown in color plate 4)

MATERIALS:

60 yards of any of the following materials:

    butcher twine

    jute twine

    rug yarn

    worsted yarn

    fine or medium-weight crochet

     cotton

    rattail yarn

appropriate size hook for yarn being used (see chart, chapter 1)

$\frac{3}{4}''$, $1''$, or $1\frac{1}{2}''$ plastic or metal rings, depending on the size of the pot

Left: Crocheted rings planter with braids extending from bottom of every ring, tied together to form a tassel. Right: Crocheted rings planter with top braids only.

Following instructions in chapter 2 for the Crocheted Rings Jewelry, crochet over and sew together very securely as many rings as are necessary to fit around the pot below the rim. It is essential that the circle of rings should remain below the pot's rim. Therefore, if the circle is too loose, leave out one ring so that it will encircle the pot's center instead (Figure 1).

Figure 1

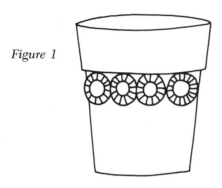

Figure 2

Braided Strings for the Bottom of the Pot

Cut 3 strands, each 26″ long. Insert all 3 through a ring, fold them in half, and braid all 6 strands together as shown in Figure 2, having 2 strands in every braiding section. Braid the strands to 3″ from the bottom. Make an overhand knot to tie the braid. Then make a braid in every ring or every other ring around, as desired. Place the circle of rings on the pot. Hold all strings together and, using a 24″ strand, make a wrapped knot as shown in chapter 1 around all the braids. The knot should fall at the center of the pot's base. Open the braids up to the wrapped knot to form a fringe.

Braided Strings for Hanging the Planter

Insert 3 strands, each 56″ long, in the top of any ring. Fold them in half and braid them to the very top. Make two or three more such braided strings, distributing them evenly around. Place the pot into the holder. Hold all strings evenly and insert their ends into a plastic or metal ring. Fold their ends over the ring and with a 36″ strand make a wrapped knot to fasten all the strands together below the ring, following instructions for the wrapped knot in chapter 1.

Bargello Planter

(As shown in color plate 6)

MATERIALS:
- a large tin can
- piece of 5-mesh or 10-mesh canvas, to measure 2″ longer than circumference of can and 2″ longer than height of can
- appropriate yarn for canvas being used (see chapter 1)
- tapestry needle
- white glue
- ¼ yard of felt

Measure the circumference and the height of the can. Add ¾″ to the circumference. Mark out those dimensions on the canvas, leaving a

1″ allowance beyond all lines. Choose a bargello pattern from among the bargello patterns shown in any of the chapters.

Work the pattern on the canvas so the rows run either horizontally or vertically, as desired (Figure 1). Fill up the total area within the lines.

Fold back and baste the seam allowance on one short end. Block the piece, stretching it slightly since it may have shrunk during stitching. Fit the piece on the can, pulling it so it fits snugly all around, and overlap the hemmed edge over the other edge. While the piece is on the can, pin the overlapped edge and hem it down over the other edge (Figure 2).

Fold the top raw edge of canvas into the can (Figure 3). Glue a strip of felt all around the inside top edge of the can, covering the canvas and part of the can. Clip the bottom raw edge of canvas many times all around, as in Figure 4. Fold the edge back onto the base of the can. Glue the canvas down all around. Cut a circle of felt, the same size as the can's base, and glue it to the bottom of the can, covering the canvas.

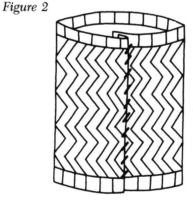

Figure 2

Figure 1

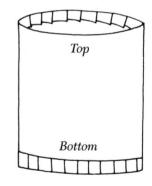

Figure 3

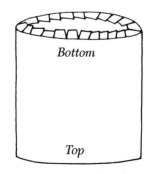

Figure 4

Four-Cord Macrame Hanging Planter

MATERIALS:
    40 yards of any of the following:
            jute twine
            butcher twine
            rattail yarn
            cable cord
    a 2″ metal ring
    knotting board and pins

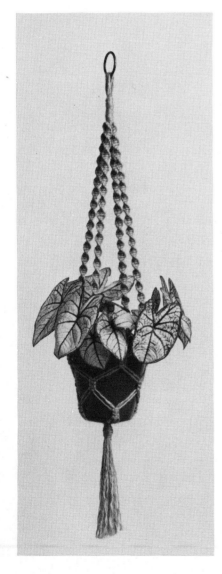

Cut the 40 yards into the following lengths:
   four 3-yard strands
   four 6½-yard strands
   two 1-yard strands

Fold the 4-yard and 6½-yard strands in half to determine their centers. Pin the centers of the two shorter strands to the board. Then pin one long strand on each side of the shorter strands. Beginning 4″ from the center points, and knotting with the longer strands, work half knots around the shorter strands for 16″. Then work a 16″ long half knot strip on the other side, again starting 4″ from the center (Figure 1).

Make an identical section with the other four strands. Hold both sections together, matching the 8″ unknotted length, and fold all the strands in the center. Insert the metal ring so that it rests in the fold. Using a 1-yard strand, and following instructions for making a wrapped knot in chapter 1, begin wrapping 2″ from the fold and end at the beginning of the half knot strips (Figure 2). Compare the lengths of the half knot strips to make sure they are even. If necessary, add or subtract knots. Then work the second step of a square knot on the end of each half knot strip.

Cradle of the Planter

Step 1: Measure the circumference of the pot at the rim. Divide that number by 8. The resulting figure will be the distance between the last knot made and the next knot. Using 2 strands from one strip and 2 strands from the adjacent strip, tie a square knot the required distance down (Figure 3). Follow with 2 more square knots close together. Do the same with the remaining 12 strands, taking 2 strands from one strip and 2 strands from the adjacent strip, and making 3 square knots on each section.

Step 2: Measure the circumference of the pot's center. Divide it by 8 to determine the distance between the last knot made and the next knot. Using 2 strands from one section and 2 strands from the adjacent section, work 3 square knots the required distance down. Work the other sections the same way. (*Note:* Be sure you are always knotting adjacent sections.)

Step 3: Measure the circumference of the pot 1″ from the base. Divide it by 8 to determine the distance between the last knot made and the next knot. Knot 4 new sections the required distance down, the same way as in Step 2.

Step 4: Place the macrame piece on the pot. Determine where to tie all strands together at the base of the pot. The bottom of the half knot strips should fall at the rim of the pot. Take the macrame piece off and make a wrapped knot the required distance down. Trim all 16 strands to an even length, 6″ from the knot.

Figure 1

Short Strands

Long Strands

8″

Center

Figure 2

Figure 3

Crocheted Striped Flowerpot Cover

(As shown in color plate 5)

This cover is designed for a conical flower pot.

MATERIALS:
    2 ounces of each of 3 or 4 colors in any of the
      following:
           synthetic or natural straw
           rug yarn
           worsted yarn
           sport yarn
           medium-weight crochet cotton
    appropriate size hook for yarn being used (see
      chart, chapter 1)

Bottom

In color A, crochet the bottom the same way as the bottom of the Crocheted Bottle Cover in the preceding chapter, working the rounds until the crocheted piece fully covers the bottom of the pot (Figure 1). At the end of the last round, slip stitch into the first single crochet stitch made on that round.

Figure 1

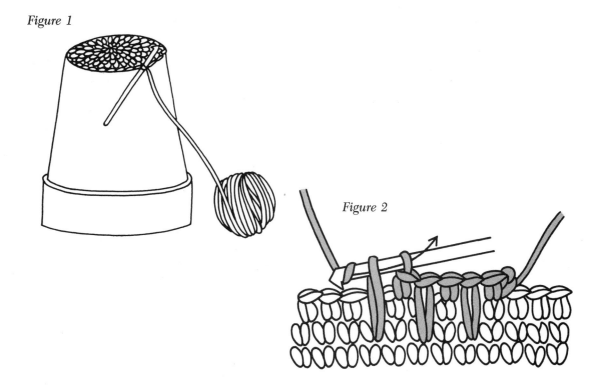

Figure 2

Fancy Stripe Pattern for Body of Planter

Round 1: Ch 1, sc in joining st, sc in each st around. Sl st in first sc made.

Rounds 2 & 3: Repeat Round 1. Fasten off Color A.

Round 4: Attach Color B in any sc, ch 1, sc in same st, *skip next st, work a sc st *loosely* 2 rows down below the skipped sc, work a sc in next st on Round 3; repeat from * around (Figure 2). The last st of the round should be a long sc st. Sl st into the first sc made.

Round 5: (*Note:* On this round, 4 sts must be increased. Count the number of sts around. Divide that number by 4 to determine where to place the increases.) Ch 1, 2 sc in joining st of last round (this is first increase made), sc in every st around, while increasing 1 sc, by working 2 sts in one st, at each of three more points. Sl st into first sc made.

Rounds 6 & 7: Repeat Round 1. Fasten off Color B.

Attach Color C in any sc of Round 7 and repeat Rounds 4 to 7. Then continue to work as many stripes as are necessary to cover the pot to the rim. Weave all the ends through the back of the stitches.

Macrame Double-Decker Hanging Planter

THIS PLANTER CAN be made plain or beaded. It is designed to accomodate two small pots hung together but can be varied quite easily. If you wish to use larger pots, simply cut each strand longer and tie more knots on each section to make the holder longer. If you wish to make a holder for one pot, cut each strand half the length that is specified.

MATERIALS:

    38 yards of any of the following:

        jute twine

        rattail

        butcher twine

        cable cord

        rug yarn

    knotting board and pins

    24 round beads for beaded planter

Cut the 38 yards into the following lengths:

    six 5½-yard lengths

    three 1-yard lengths

    one 2-yard length

Holding all six long strands evenly, fold them in half to determine their centers. Fold the 2-yard strand in half and place its center across the centers of the six strands. Work 13 half hitch knots with one end of the tying strand (End A, Figure 1). Then tie 13 knots with end B (Figure 2). Fold the knotted section in half to form a large loop.

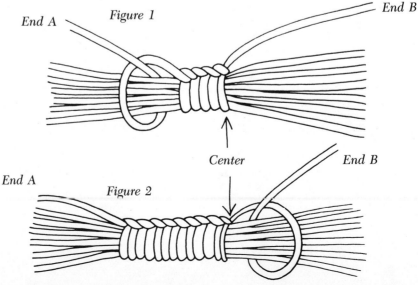

End A   *Figure 1*   End B

Center

End A   *Figure 2*   End B

Using one 1-yard strand, and following instructions in chapter 1 for making a wrapped knot, wrap it tightly around all 14 strands ten times. Clip the four ends of the tying and wrapping strands close to the knot.

Note: Before proceeding with the rest of the knotting, gather each strand and fasten it with a rubber band for ease of working, as shown in chapter 1.

Knotting Pattern for Unbeaded Planter

Divide the 12 strands into 3 groups of 4 strands each. Working on one 4-strand section at a time, tie a square knot $2\frac{1}{2}''$ from the bottom of the wrapped knot, then tie a square knot every $2\frac{1}{2}''$ (Figure 3) until there are 5 square knots made. Work the other sections the same way, making sure that the spacings between the knots are identical with the first section. The last knot on each section should be about 13″ from the bottom of the wrapped knot.

Knotting Pattern for the Beaded Planter

Divide the 12 strands into 3 groups of 4 strands each. Working on one section, make 2 square knots 4 inches from the wrapped knot. Insert a bead on the anchor cords and make 2 more square knots. Then follow Figure 4, inserting 4 beads in all, and making 2 square knots after the last bead. Make one more square knot 13″ from the wrapped knot. Work the other two sections the same way.

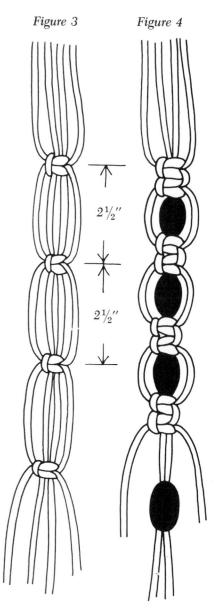

Figure 3 Figure 4

$2\frac{1}{2}''$

$2\frac{1}{2}''$

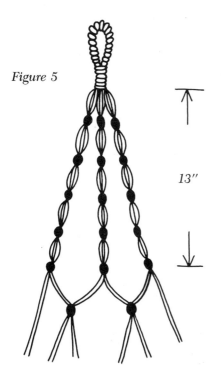

Figure 5

13″

Cradle of the Upper Pot

Step 1: Measure the circumference of the pot at the rim. Divide that amount by 6. The resulting figure will be the distance between the last knot made and the next knot. Using 2 strands from one section and 2 strands from the adjacent section tie a square knot the required distance down. Do the same with the remaining 8 strands, taking 2 strands from one section and 2 strands from the adjacent section, and making 1 square knot.

Step 2: Measure the circumference of the pot about 1″ up from the bottom of the pot. Divide it by 6. The resulting number is the distance between the last knot made and the next knot. Using 2 strands from one section and 2 strands from the adjacent section, work a square knot the required distance down. Work the other sections the same way.

Step 3: Measure the diameter of the bottom of the pot. Divide it by 2 to determine the radius. Using another 1-yard strand, wrap it around all 12 strands 10 times, very tightly. The distance from the last knot made and the beginning of the wrapped knot should be the same length as the radius. Fasten the wrapping strand and clip off the ends.

Lower Pot

Divide the 12 strands into 3 sections and work the same knot pattern as for the upper pot. The cradle, too, is formed the same way. Once all the knotting and the last wrapped knot are made, trim all the ends to an even length of 6″.

Appliquéd Flower Pot

Figure 1

(As shown in color plate 3)

MATERIALS:

    a clay or plastic flower pot, or a tin can of any
      size
    white (milk-base) glue
    varnish or clear polyurethane finish used to coat
      wood
    scraps of cotton fabric, preferably calico prints
    brush

Figure 2

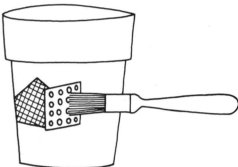

Making a Crazy-Quilt Pot (Figure 1)

Cut odd-shaped pieces of fabric. Dilute the glue with water to a milky consistency. Brush the glue on one part of the pot. Place a piece of fabric on this area and brush glue on top of it (Figure 2). Then place another piece alongside the first, overlapping it slightly. Brush it over with glue. Continue in this manner, applying the glue to the pot and then to the fabric, and placing the pieces to conform to the pot's shape. The pieces at the top of the pot should be folded over the rim to extend inside the pot. Allow the glue to dry, then apply a coat or two of varnish for a glaze.

Figure 3

Making a Floral-Motif Appliquéd Pot (Figure 3)

To obtain this effect, use a bright colored plastic pot. (Refer to page 109 for the Floral Motif pattern.) Make a template for the petal and center pieces, cutting away the seam allowance. Cut 8 petals and 1 center. Using the same technique as for the crazy-quilt pot, glue the center of the flower to the pot first, then each petal, the edges touching each other but not overlapping. The top of the pot could be done in a crazy-quilt pattern using the same calico prints used for the motif. Once dry, glaze the entire pot.

5 ——————— Wall Decorations

Left: Patchwork pattern made into a hanging, with supporting dowels at top and bottom, and hanger made from matching fabric. Right: Patchwork pattern made into a picture; fabric is stretched around cardboard and framed.

In this chapter you will discover a number of solutions to the problem of how to decorate the walls in your home. Most large wall areas—such as those above sofas, beds, and dining areas—require big, bold pieces. By using the techniques explained in this chapter you will be able to make these large wall decorations in a short time.

Shown is a method of covering fabric with crocheted appliqués to create wall hangings. Large, bold, and graphic wall decorations are made by sewing together fabric squares and triangles to form patterns. Small quilts for hanging, miniatures of those used to cover beds, are made with simple appliqué techniques.

For decorating small wall areas you can choose from any of the more diminutive designs made with more refined craft techniques. There is a selection of miniature pictures to embroider, an assortment of macrame hangings to knot, and ideas for using the bargello method of canvas-work to create colorful hangings and pictures.

Patchwork Wall Decorations

THOUGH THE TECHNIQUE of patchwork has traditionally been used for making quilts, consider how attractive and eye-catching a symmetrically patterned patchwork square would look hung on a wall. (See color plate 5.)

Unlike most patchwork quilts, which are constructed with a variety of different shapes, each of the three distinct patchwork squares featured here is built from multiples of only two basic shapes—a square and a triangle.

Squares and triangles are very easy shapes to sew together. A patchwork wall decoration, designed to cover a 20″ x 20″ expanse of wall space, can be completed in a short time. Of course, a lot depends on whether it is made by machine or by hand. The advantages of machine sewing are speed and a crisp, contemporary look; a patchwork piece will have a charming antique look if sewn by hand.

A patchwork wall decoration can contain leftover scraps from fabric used for making curtains or a bedspread for the same room, thus creating a coordinated look. Though calico, gingham, and other solid and printed cotton fabrics are most commonly used for patchwork, do not overlook the possibility of combining different colors of corduroy, velveteen, satin, or all three together in one piece.

Besides their use as wall decorations, individual patchwork squares can be made into large knife-edge pillows, as shown in chapter 3; or one part of the patchwork pattern can be sewn as an appliqué onto a store-bought pillow. When these same squares are made in multiples, they can be sewn together to form quilts (explained further in this chapter), as well as shower curtains, kitchen curtains, and tablecloths.

MATERIALS:

    3 or 4 contrasting solid color or printed fabrics,
       ¼ yard of each
    sewing needle and thread (if constructing piece
       by hand)

Following instructions in chapter 1, make a template for the square and triangle patterns. Choose any one of the three patchwork patterns. Cut the required number of squares, triangles, and strips in each color, as specified.

The edging strips are sewn on once all the small pieces are attached together. The patchwork square should be put together one

Figure 1

152 / *Wall Decorations*

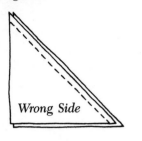

Wrong Side

Figure 2

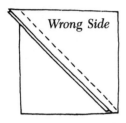

Wrong Side

Figure 3

vertical panel at a time, starting with the first panel at left. To begin, sew all the triangles of the first panel together to form squares, following the chart. Place one triangle over the other, right sides facing, and join together the longest sides of the two (Figure 1). Fold the seam to one side (Figure 2). On the right side baste the seam down, using small stitches, and if available, a matching color thread (Figure 3). If you wish, simply press it to one side.

Then sew all the squares of the first panel together, following the chart. Fold each seam to one side, and baste it down on the right side (Figure 4).

Work the second panel the same way, then attach it to the first (Figure 5), matching all seams. Finish the seams with basting (Figure 6).

Continue in this manner, working each panel separately and attaching it to the others. Once the square is formed, sew the two short strips to two opposing sides of the square. Baste their seams down. Then sew the two long strips to the two remaining edges of the square, forming an even edging all around.

Stretch the patchwork piece over a square of cardboard which measures 2″ less in height and in width than the fabric. Tape the raw edges to the back of the mounting board. Then frame the hanging if desired, or hang it unframed.

Figure 4

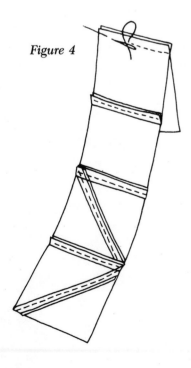

Figure 5

Figure 6

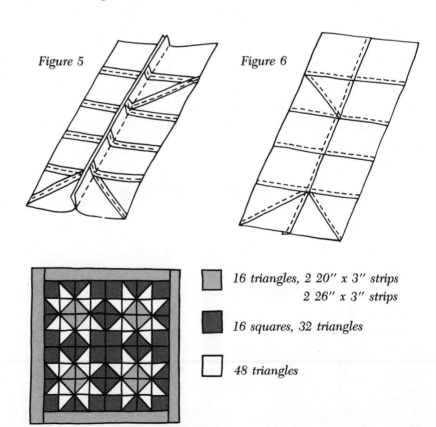

16 triangles, 2 20″ x 3″ strips
2 26″ x 3″ strips

16 squares, 32 triangles

48 triangles

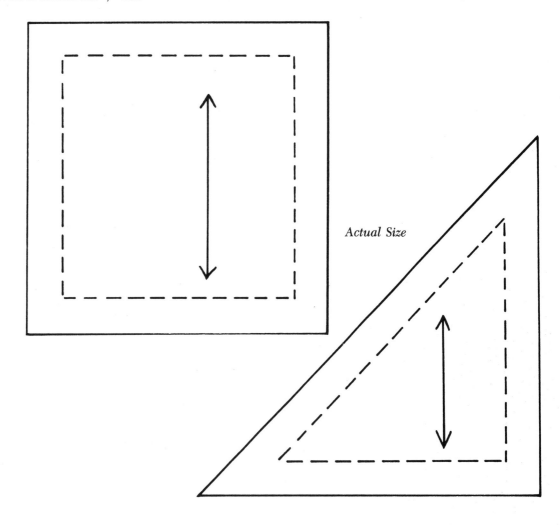

Actual Size

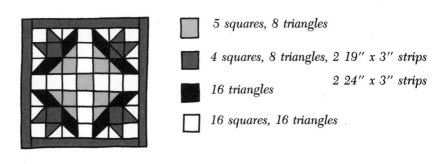

5 squares, 8 triangles

4 squares, 8 triangles, 2 19" x 3" strips

2 24" x 3" strips

16 triangles

16 squares, 16 triangles

8 squares, 4 triangles, 2 19" x 4" strips

2 26" x 4" strips

12 triangles, 1 square

8 squares, 12 triangles

16 squares, 4 triangles

Crocheted Wall Hangings

MAKING A FULLY crocheted wall hanging is as ambitious and as time-consuming a project as crocheting an afghan. By crocheting only certain parts of the hanging and combining these parts with fabric, you can still create a striking wall decoration investing only a fraction of your time and effort.

Done in the *granny square* technique of working from the center and building the piece round by round, floral motifs are easy appliqués to construct. Scraps of all kinds of yarn can be utilized, since each round of the flower requires very little yarn. The floral motif can look just as effective, though differing in size, when crocheted in worsted yarn, rug yarn, mohair, jute, or other threads. For an unusual multi-textured hanging, consider unconventional combinations of yarn in one motif, such as metallics and wool, or straw and mohair.

In making a crocheted hanging, it is best to first crochet a sample motif in order to know the dimensions of the flower when done in your choice of yarn. These figures will enable you to design the hanging and determine how large a piece of fabric to use for the background, how many appliqués it will have, and how they will be arranged. The hanging appearing in the color plate measures 18″ by 22″. All the motifs for the hanging have been crocheted with two strands of worsted yarn, using a size J aluminum crochet hook. The appliqués for the matching afghan and pillow were crocheted with one strand of the same yarn, using a size H aluminum crochet hook.

As shown in the hanging sketched, a lot of variations can be created with these crocheted appliqués. Stems and leaves do not always have to accompany the flowers, and the stems can easily be made longer or shorter. Rather than mounting the appliqués on one solid piece of fabric, you can mount each motif on a separate piece, each piece a different color. When each piece has been edged with crochet, all the separately worked parts of the hanging are joined together. In making the hanging shown, attach the three squares for either side first. Then measure the three-square panel. To make sure the panels will later fit together evenly, cut the center panel a bit shorter to allow for the crocheted edging which will make the panel longer and wider.

In other variations the crocheted edging can be dispensed with altogether. Instead, you can simply hem the raw edges of the fabric, or bind the fabric all around with bias binding in a contrasting color.

154

Wall Hanging with Crocheted Appliqués

(As shown in color plate 2)

MATERIALS:

piece of felt, burlap, or other material for the background

scraps of yarn in several colors plus green, in any of the following:

worsted yarn

sport yarn

rug yarn

raffia or synthetic straw

fine or medium-weight crochet cotton

crochet hook in appropriate size for yarn being used (See chart, chapter 1)

sewing needle and sewing thread, for sewing appliqués

hole puncher for making holes into edges of fabric, if felt is used as background

2 dowels, curtain rods, branches, or other poles on which to mount the hanging

Crocheting the Floral Appliqué

When crocheted in worsted yarn, the length of the flower and stem is 9½ inches.

Flower

Round 1: In Color A ch 5, sl st in first ch to form ring, ch 3, 11 dc into ring. Sl st in third ch of ch-3 (Figure 1). Fasten off.

Figure 1

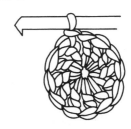

Round 2: Attach Color B in any dc, ch 3, dc in same st, 2 dc in next st and in every st around. Sl st in third ch of ch-3 (Figure 2). Fasten off. (24 dc around).

Round 3: Attach Color C in any dc,*(1 sc, 1 hdc, 1 dc) in next st, 3 trc in next st, (1 dc, 1 hdc, 1 sc) in next st (Figure 3); repeat from * five times. Sl st in sp where yarn was attached. Fasten off.

Figure 2

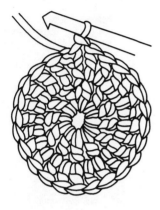

Stem

With Green ch 25, sc in second ch from hook and in every one of the next 23 chs. Work 3 more sc sts in last ch. Working on the other side of the original chain, work a sc st in every ch across (Figure 4). Fasten off.

(*Note:* The length of the stem can be adjusted for the design by making more or fewer chains than specified.)

Leaf

(Make 2, 4 or 6, depending on the design desired and the length of the stem.)

Figure 4

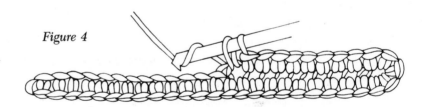

Figure 3

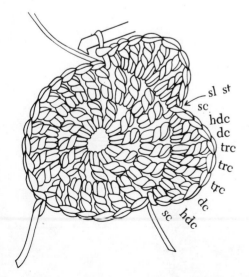

sl st
sc
hdc
dc
trc
trc
trc
dc
sc hdc

Figure 5

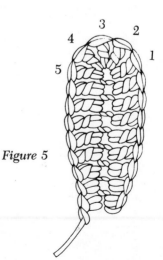

3
4   2
5   1

With Green ch 10, work a sc in second ch from hook, sc in third ch, hdc in fourth ch, dc in each of next 6 chs; work 4 more dc in last ch. Working on the other side of the chaining row, make a dc in each of the next 5 chs, hdc in next ch, sc in last 2 chs (Figure 5). Fasten off.

Weave all the ends of all the pieces into the back of the work. Steam-press the pieces lightly to flatten them.

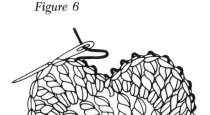

Figure 6

Attaching Appliqués to the Fabric

Arrange and pin the flowers, stems, and leaves on the fabric. Using cotton or polyester thread in a neutral color, sew the pieces to the fabric with small stitches, as in Figure 6.

Border Edging

If felt is used for the background, punch holes all around ½″ apart, ⅜″ from the edge, using a hole puncher. If a woven fabric is used, make a ¼″ hem all around, basting it down. If the fabric is closely-woven, use a small, sharp, steel crochet hook, such as size 2, for crocheting the first round of the edging. Pierce the fabric with the hook and crochet rather loosely.

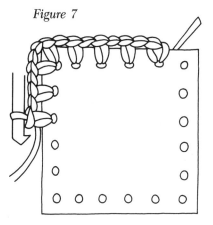

Figure 7

Round 1: Attach any color yarn in any hole, ch 1, sc in same sp,*ch 1, sc in next hole; repeat from * to the corner. In the corner hole work (sc, ch 2, sc) (Figure 7). Work all the other sides and the other three corners the same way. At the end of the round, sl st into the first sc st made. Fasten off.

Round 2: Attach a second color in any ch-1 sp, sc in same sp, *sc in next sc, sc in next ch-1 sp; repeat from * to the corner ch-2 sp. In the corner sp work (sc, ch 2, sc). Work all the other sides and corners the same way. At the end of the round sl st into the first sc made. Fasten off.

Repeat Round 2 as many times and in as many colors as desired. When done, steam-press the hanging, flattening it and being careful not to stretch it out of shape.

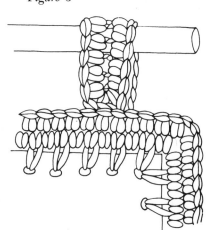

Figure 8

Carriers for the Dowels

In any one of the colors, ch 12. Work the same way as for the stem, making sc sts on either side of the chaining row. Fasten off, leaving a 10″ end. Use this end to sew the folded carrier piece to the back edge of the border, as shown in Figure 8. Make as many carriers as are necessary to support the dowels on the top and on the bottom.

Macrame Wall Hangings

WE CAN ALL appreciate the beauty of a large, complex macrame hanging containing a variety of intricate knots. The "natural look" in home decor is in vogue, and a macrame hanging made of a natural fiber like jute can complement rooms decorated in any of the styles from early American to more contemporary rattan.

Few people have the time or patience to construct monumental macrame pieces. Neither is it wise for beginners to attempt such projects. Presented here are ideas for macrame hangings that anyone can attempt and complete.

Each of the three strips is made with basic, easy-to-do knots. Of course, all the knots should be learned and practiced first, using scrap ropes. Any one of these three strips, when mounted from a ring as shown in Figures 1 and 2, or from a small dowel, can serve as individual, complete hangings for small, narrow wall areas. The challenge, though, is in forming larger hangings which are combinations of a few strips (Figure 3). Though the hangings are most effective created from one color of jute or other material, experimenting with making each of the strips a different color, or even making each strip multicolor, could produce exciting effects.

Hanging made from multicolor necklace pattern (chapter 2).

Figure 1

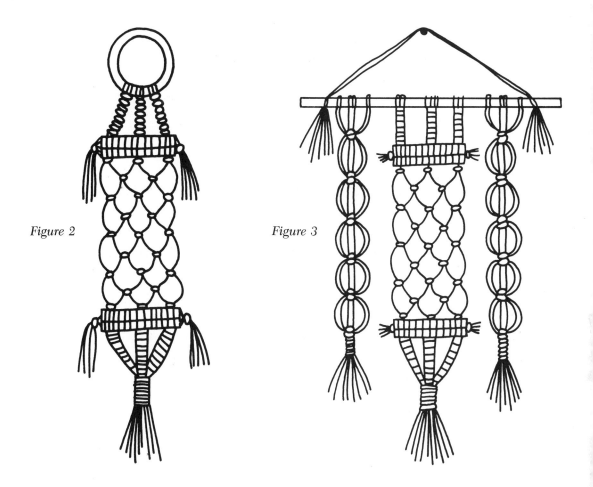

Figure 2

Figure 3

In addition to wall decorations, other applications can be found for these strips. By initially cutting and mounting longer strands, and thereby making longer strips, you can construct ceiling to floor room dividers from multiples of one or two strip patterns. By mounting the strands on a curtain rod instead of a dowel before knotting, you can create an unusual window panel. By mounting many bright colors of rug yarn or very thick gift wrapping yarn on a painted wooden ring or dowel, and then knotting them in strips, you can make a colorful mobile for a child's crib.

Besides using the three strip patterns featured here for any wall hanging project, you can also consider using the knotting patterns of the Beaded Choker and Multicolor Necklace in chapter 2, or any of the macrame planter patterns in chapter 4. With a little imagination, you could combine the different basic knots shown in chapter 1 to form original strip patterns.

MATERIALS FOR ALL STRIPS:
>   the specified number of yards of any of the
>   following:
>   jute twine
>   rattail
>   butcher twine
>   rug yarn
>   cable cord
>   gift wrapping yarn
>   knotting board and pins
>   ½" diameter wood dowel, flat wood strip, ring,
>   or other decorative piece on which to mount
>   the strips

Note: If knotted in jute twine, each strip will measure approximately 22 inches long and will have the same number of pattern repeats as the sketches of the wall hangings indicate.

Strip One

(See color plate 4)

Cut 17 yards into the following lengths:
   two 3½-yard strands
   two 4½-yard strands
   one 36-inch strand

Fold each 3½-yard strand in half and mount the fold on the dowel with a lark's head knot. Fold each 4½-yard strand in half and mount on either side of the two mounted strands. Over the four center strands work 4 square knots, knotting over the two center anchor cords. On each side work as follows: With A, work a double half hitch knot over B (Figure 1). With B work a double half hitch knot over A. Continue making double half hitch knots, alternately knotting with A over B or with B over A, until 5 knots are made. Using both A strands from either edge make 2 square knots over all six strands at center (Figure 2).

For the second repeat, work 4 square knots with the four center strands. Make 5 double half hitch knots on the 2-strand sections at left and at right, starting the knotting with strand A. Make 2 square knots over all six strands with A, completing the second repeat.

Make 4 more repeats. After the last 2 square knots done with A, wrap the 36-inch strand over all eight strands about 12 times, forming a wrapped knot. Clip the ends of the knot, then trim all strands to an even length of 6″.

Figure 1

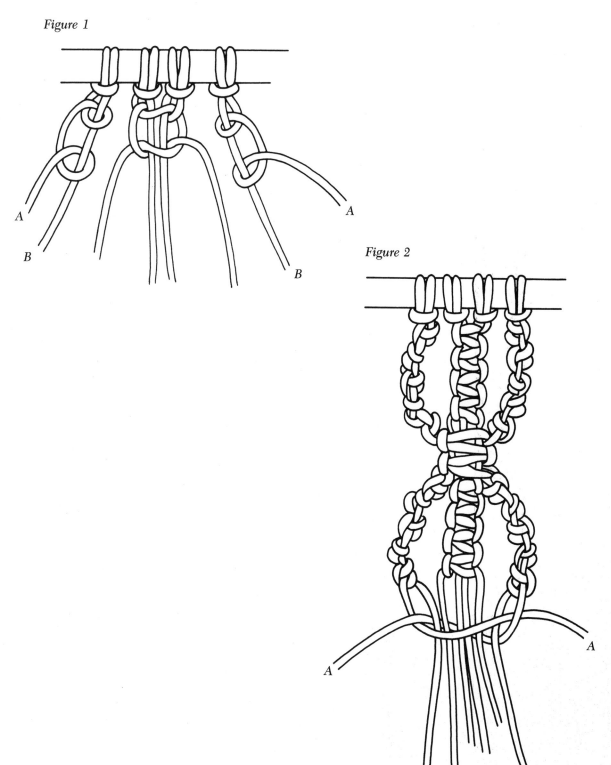

Figure 2

Strip Two

(See color plate 4)

Cut 24 yards into the following lengths:
 six $3\frac{1}{2}$-yard strands
 four 18-inch strands
 one 36-inch strand

Fold each long strand in half and mount on the dowel with a lark's head knot. Divide the 12 strands into three groups of 4 strands each. Make 5 square knots on each section. Make an overhand knot on each side of an 18-inch strand. Pin it across all 12 strands. Starting at left, make a double half hitch knot with each strand across. Pin another 18-inch strand beneath the row just made and make another double half hitch row.

Working in alternating square knot pattern make 9 rows of square knots, the rows about $\frac{3}{4}''$ apart. (Draw horizontal lines, $\frac{3}{4}''$ apart, on the knotting board, for aid in placement of the knots.) Then make 2 double half hitch rows as before, using the two other 18-inch strands.

Divide the 12 strands into three sections. Make 5 square knots on each section (Figure 1).

Using the 36-inch strand make a wrapped knot around all 12 strands, wrapping it 12 times. Trim all 12 strands to an even length of 6'' after the knot.

Tie the two ends at each edge of the double half hitch rows together with an overhand knot. Trim them to a length of 1'', or leave them long.

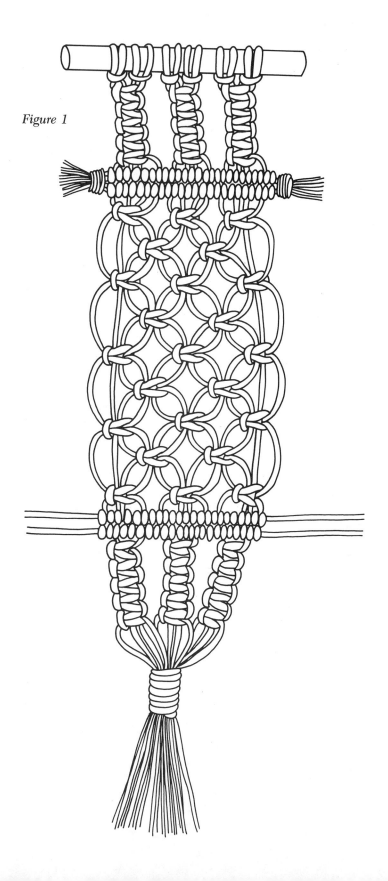

Figure 1

Strip Three

Cut 18 yards into six 3-yard strands.

Fold each strand in half and mount on the dowel with a lark's head knot. Make 3 square knots with the center four strands, working over two center anchor cords. Place a pin in each center anchor cord and extend each across diagonally over five strands in opposite directions. Make a knot on each and pin the knot to the board. Starting from the center, work double half hitch knots with each strand from the center to the left, and each strand from the center to the right. Insert a pin into each anchor cord at right and left edges after the last knots. Extend each diagonally across to the center. Starting with the strand at each edge, make a double half hitch knot with each strand to the center (Figure 1).

The original anchor cords will now again be the anchor cords for the square knots. Make 3 square knots, knotting with a strand on either side of the two anchor cords.

Continue in this manner, making 3 diamond patterns. Then make 8 square knots after the last diamond. Trim the ends of the four center strands to 4″, all the others to an even 6″ length.

Figure 1

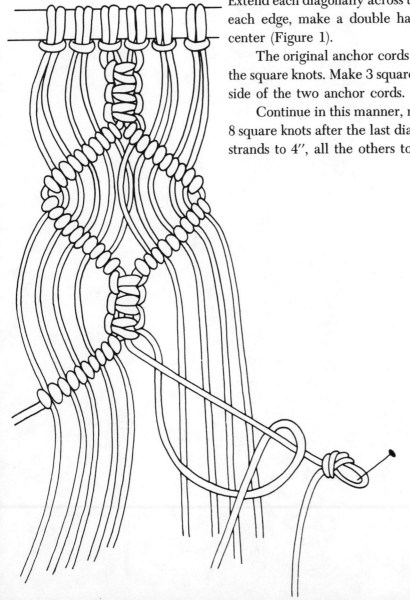

Miniature Stitcheries

A MINIATURE STITCHERY can accent a small wall area in any room of your home, from living room and bedroom to kitchen, hallway, and baby's room. Groupings of mini-stitcheries can be hung together to fill larger wall areas.

Any of the four stitchery designs presented here can be completed in one evening. Each is made with simple embroidery stitches. The colors used are bright basics—shades of red, yellow, and green—rather than unusual, hard to find shades. Any type of fabric can be used for the background, as long as the stitches can easily be embroidered on it with your choice of yarn. Recommended, though, is linen or hopsacking in any color.

Two attractive ways of framing and displaying the mini-stitcheries are shown. The floral bouquet is permanently mounted on a painted embroidery hoop; the three smaller embroideries are framed with an oval fabric mat. Other imaginative ideas for displaying these mini-stitcheries: sewing the three fabric-matted pieces together to form a horizontal or a vertical rectangular hanging; framing the floral bouquet in a circular fabric mat and mounting it onto a large, round embroidery hoop; or embroidering any of these designs as accents on pillows, quilts, and pot holders.

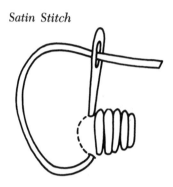

Satin Stitch

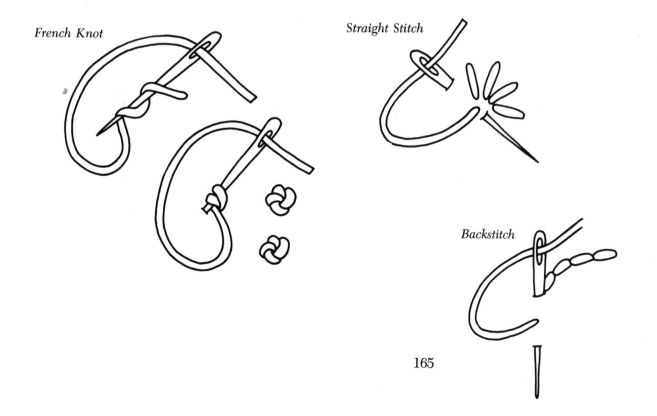

French Knot

Straight Stitch

Backstitch

165

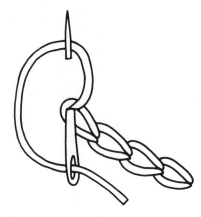

Chain Stitch

General Instructions · for all Stitcheries

MATERIALS:

> 12″ square of linen or hopsacking in white, ecru, or desired color
> 1 ounce of each color specified in either 3-strand crewel yarn or 6-strand embroidery floss
> small embroidery hoop for the 3 miniatures; 7″ diameter round hoop for the Floral Bouquet
> embroidery needle

Trace the design on the *heavy* lines. Following instructions in chapter 1 transfer the design to the fabric. Stretch the fabric on an embroidery hoop.

In following the diagram and the instructions the letters refer to the colors, the numbers indicate the stitch. The fine lines indicate the direction of the stitches. Use 1 strand of crewel yarn or 3 strands of embroidery floss unless otherwise indicated.

Split Stitch

Lazy Daisy Stitch
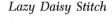

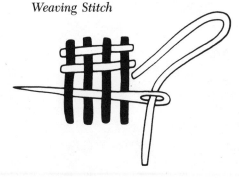

Weaving Stitch

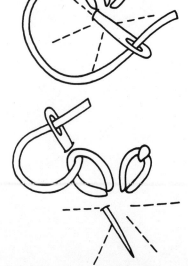

Floral Bouquet

(As shown in color plate 8)

Colors

A—Yellow
B—Orange
C—Brown
D—Rust
E—Lilac
F—Light Green
G—Dark Green

Stitches

1—Satin Stitch
2—Split Stitch
3—Straight Stitch
4—French Knot

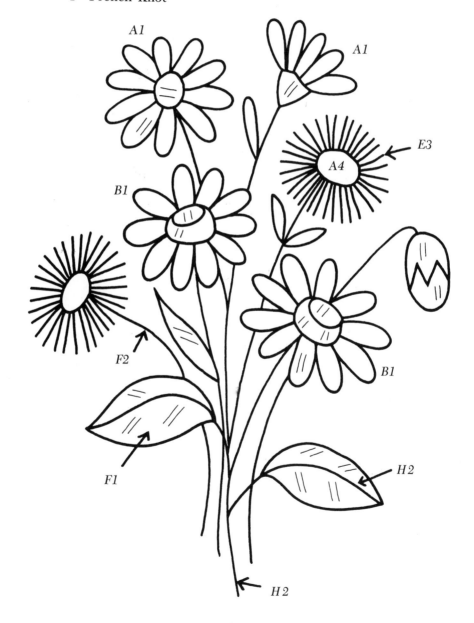

Working Procedure

1—Work the petals of the orange flowers in orange satin stitch.

2—Work the petals of the yellow flower and bud in yellow satin stitch; work a few french knots in yellow in the centers of the lilac flowers.

3—Make a few brown satin stitches in the centers of the yellow and orange flowers; complete orange flower centers by working rust satin stitches around the brown centers.

4—Work straight stitches for the petals of the lilac flowers in lilac.

5—Work the stems and veins of leaves of the orange flowers using dark green split stitch.

6—Work all the other stems in light green split stitch; work all the leaves in satin stitch, in direction specified.

Framing the Stitchery

Block and frame the completed stitchery in a 6″ by 8″ frame. Or, stretch it on a 7″ embroidery hoop, centering the design. Cut the excess fabric all around so that a ¾″ edge remains beyond the hoop. Clip the edge all around. Using white glue, fold back and glue the edge to the back of the inside part of the hoop. Allow it to dry. Unfasten the outer hoop. Take out the screw and nut. Paint the wood in any color desired. Glue it around the other ring, with the opening at the top of the design. Pull a string or yarn through the two holes at top. Tie the two ends of the string together and form it into a hanger by which to hang the stitchery.

Basket of Apples

(As shown in color plate 8)

Colors

A—Red
B—Cranberry
C—Green
D—Brown
E—Gold

Stitches

1—Satin Stitch
2—Chain Stitch
3—Split Stitch
4—Backstitch
5—Weaving

Working Procedure

1—Using 2 strands of crewel yarn, or 6 strands of embroidery floss, in gold, lay vertical rows in direction specified on both sides of basket. Using 1 strand of brown, weave across through the gold strands in the opposite direction. Brown rows should be ⅛″ apart, and weaving should be done on one side of basket at a time.

2—Outline bottom and sides of basket in brown split stitch. Work all stems of apples in brown split stitch.

3—Work rim of basket in gold split stitch.

4—Thread needle with 1 strand of gold and 1 strand of brown. Work handle of basket in gold chain stitch.

5—Work all red apples in red satin stitch. Work all other apples in cranberry.

6—Outline each apple in brown backstitch.

7—Work 2 or 3 satin stitches in green for each leaf.

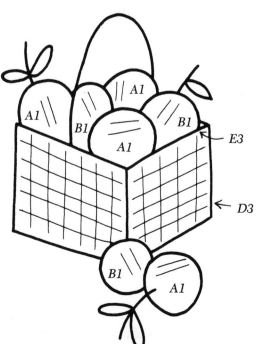

House in the Woods

(As shown in color plate 8)

Colors

A—Brown
B—Red
C—Orange
D—Gold
E—Green

Stitches

1—Split Stitch
2—Satin Stitch
3—French Knot
4—Lazy Daisy Stitch
5—Straight Stitch

Working Procedure

1—Outline tree trunk, branches, house, and path leading to house, and horizon line in brown split stitch; fill in roof of left side of house in brown satin stitch.

2—Work chimney and roof of house in red satin stitch; work petals of flower in foreground in red lazy daisy stitch.

3—Using 2 strands of crewel yarn, or 6 strands of embroidery floss, work green french knots on the dots for the leaves of the tree; work stems of flowers in split stitch, leaves and grass in green straight stitch.

4—Make window and house door in gold satin stitch; outline both in brown straight stitch; make gold french knots in centers of flowers.

5—Work small flower in orange straight stitch; large orange flower is done in lazy daisy stitch.

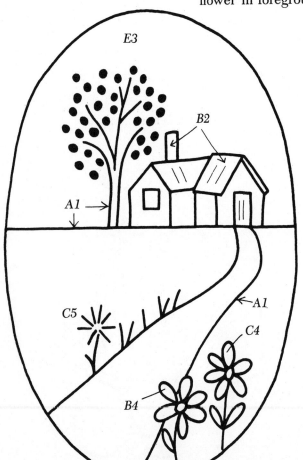

Owl on a Branch

(As shown in color plate 8)

Colors

A—Brown
B—Gold
C—Red
D—Orange
E—Dark Green

Stitches

1—Satin Stitch
2—Split Stitch
3—Lazy Daisy Stitch
4—Straight Stitch

Working Procedure

1—Outline head of owl, eyes, and feathers on each outer edge in brown split stitch; work satin stitch for the inner eye, each side of head, as indicated.

2—Work gold satin stitch for head, beak, feet; work gold split stitch next to brown row on each side of feathers.

3—Work red split stitch for inside of eye, next to brown row; work a red row next to gold row on feathers.

4—Work two green split stitch rows for branch.

5—Work an orange lazy daisy stitch on each oval feather of body; make a brown straight stitch into each lazy daisy stitch.

Finishing the Miniatures

Make a pattern for the oval frame for each stitchery by tracing the oval encircling the House in the Woods design. Trace it onto a matching

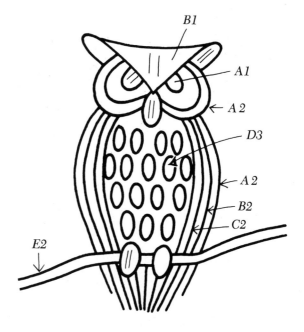

calico print. Cut out the inside of the oval $\frac{1}{4}''$ in from the line. Clip the $\frac{1}{4}''$ edge all around as shown in Figure 1. Turn the edge back and baste it. Place the oval mat on the stitchery, centering the design. Using small stitches, hem the mat to the embroidered fabric. Frame the completed piece in a 5″ x 7″ frame.

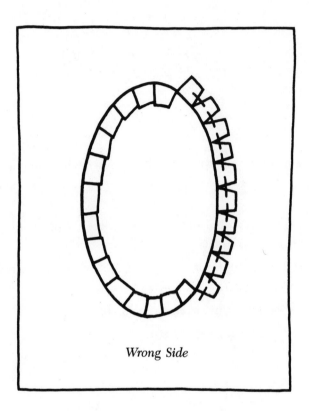

Wrong Side

Bargello Pictures and Hangings

SINCE THE TECHNIQUE of bargello consists of long stitches that cover many holes of needlepoint canvas at one time, it allows you to complete a picture or a wall hanging in a short time.

Rather than stitching on 10-mesh canvas that you use for making small accessories and pillows, you can use canvas with larger holes and stitch with proportionately heavier yarn. All the bargello patterns shown in chapter 1 can be utilized for making hangings. With a little imagination you can combine two or more patterns to form very unusual designs. The hanging shown in color plate 6, done in earth tones, achieves the "Navajo rug" look through the combination of two patterns—the Paperback Book Cover and the Diamond Patterned Pillow. Plate 3 shows a hanging which is coordinated with the pillow. Both are done in the same bargello design, but the hanging is twice as large because of the use of 5-mesh canvas rather than the 10-mesh canvas used for the pillow.

Diamond-shaped pillow appliqué done in rug yarn on 5-mesh canvas, nailed to fabric-covered board, and framed.

General Instructions

MATERIALS

30″ x 30″ piece of 5-mesh canvas, or size required

various colors of rug yarn

tapestry needle with very large eye

Choose any bargello pattern desired. Using a *double strand* of rug yarn, work the stitches in any design or combination of designs. Fold back and baste the raw edges of the completed piece. Hem the piece to felt or other fabric, or stretch it on a mounting board and frame it. Another possibility for displaying it is to nail it to a larger piece of stained wood, letting the wood form a frame around it.

Navajo Wall Hanging

(As shown in color plate 6)

MATERIALS:
  15″ x 20″ piece of 5-mesh duo canvas
  2 ounces of rug yarn in each of the following
    colors:
      Brown, Rust, Gold, and Off-White
        two 16″ long ³⁄₈″ dowels

Bargello Patterns Used

Diamond Appliqué for Pillow, page 126
Paperback Book Cover, page 181
Note: Use 2 strands of rug yarn throughout.
Following Diamond Appliqué pattern, begin at center of the canvas piece and stitch as follows:

Center Diamond: Brown

Round 1: Gold	**Round 3:** Brown
Round 2: Rust	**Round 4:** Off-White

Following the Paperback Book Cover pattern, in brown, work a Row 1 of the pattern, making one stitch above the top stitch of the diamond and 32 stitches on either side. Work the zigzag pattern above the Brown row as follows:

Another **Row 1** of pattern in Gold

Row 2: Rust	**Row 4:** Rust
Row 3: Off-White	**Row 5:** Gold

Another **Row 1** of pattern in Brown

Work the same zigzag pattern on the bottom of the diamond. Following the diamond pattern again, fill in each unworked section on either side of the diamond, ending the stitching to follow the outlines of the piece.

Round 5: Gold	**Round 8:** Rust
Round 6: Off-White	**Round 9:** Gold
Round 7: Brown	**Round 10:** Brown

Navajo wall hanging.

Fill in each unworked triangle at the four corners with long vertical stitches in Off-White.

Fold back and hem the edges of the canvas. Following instructions given for the Crocheted Wall Hanging, make six dowel carriers. Or, make dowel carriers by folding 3″ long strips of matching color bias binding in half. Sew them to the top and bottom edges of the piece and insert the dowels. In Rust, braid a length to measure 25″. Sew each end to the top dowel.

Miniature Quilts

THE SAME CRAFT techniques used for making bed-size quilts can be utilized to create smaller versions for use as wall hangings and baby quilts.

Quilts are usually made piecemeal. One component is constructed at a time, either by embroidering or appliquéing a square of solid color fabric with an attractive multicolor motif, or by sewing small pieces of fabric together to form a patchwork square. Then all the squares are joined together, and the entire fabric is quilted with batting or simply lined.

Several of the designs appearing in other projects can be fashioned into charming miniature quilts. The floral bouquet stitchery can be embroidered on a few squares of fabric, each square done in the same motif but each embroidered in a different color combination. The miniature stitcheries, too, would form an unusual quilt, each square consisting of an embroidery with an oval frame encircling it. Any of the patchwork patterns can be made in multiples and joined together to create a very striking patchwork pattern.

The easiest method for decorating a square is by appliquéing it, with the fabric pieces appliquéd in the "iron-on" technique. Shown in the drawing is the eight-petal floral motif translated into a miniature quilt. Calico prints applied on a neutral ground look best, but various colors of felt can also be used for each petal and center. Each multicolor motif can be appliquéd to a different color felt square. The only sewing required in creating this piece is in joining the squares together. This easy-to-make colorful felt hanging, as well as the other miniature quilts, could be a great wall decoration for a child's room, family room, bedroom, or kitchen.

Floral Motif Miniature Quilt

(As shown in color plate 1)

MATERIALS:

six 12″ x 12″ squares of any fabric, preferably a
  solid color cotton.

$\frac{1}{8}$ yard of each of nine different prints or solids

$\frac{1}{2}$ yard of matching color fabric for making
  binding, or wide bias binding

fusible webbing

24″ x 36″ piece of polyester or cotton batting

same size piece of fabric for the lining

two 26″ inch dowels or curtain rods for hanging
  quilt

Trace the pattern for the petal and center appearing on page 109.
Cut away the seam allowances. For each square of the quilt, cut 8
petals, 1 center. Using the *iron-on* technique of appliqué, apply the

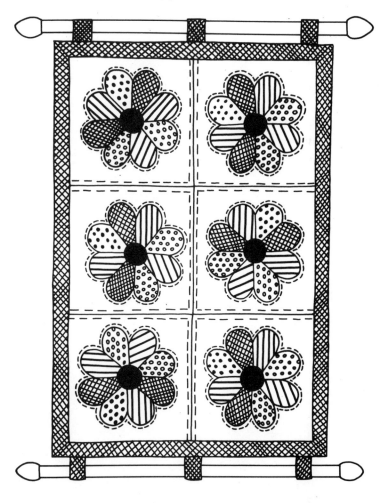

eight petals to the square first, then apply the center. Edge all the pieces with zigzagging or blanket stitch embroidery. Make six appliquéd squares. Sew them together as shown.

Quilt the piece as follows: Place the lining, wrong side up, on a flat surface. Place the batting on top of it, then the quilt top. Pin all three layers together very securely and with many pins all over. Machine-sew or hand-baste on all the seam lines, on each side of each seam, and around each flower, sewing through all three layers.

Cut 3″ bias strips out of matching fabric. Join them to form one continuous strip. On the right side, pin binding to two opposite edges of the quilt. Attach binding with a ¾″ seam (Figure 1). Fold binding to wrong side, fold under the raw edge, and hem the binding down (Figure 2). Work the other two edges the same way, trimming and folding under the excess length at each of the four corners. Make dowel carriers out of the same fabric and sew them to top and bottom edges of the quilt.

Figure 1

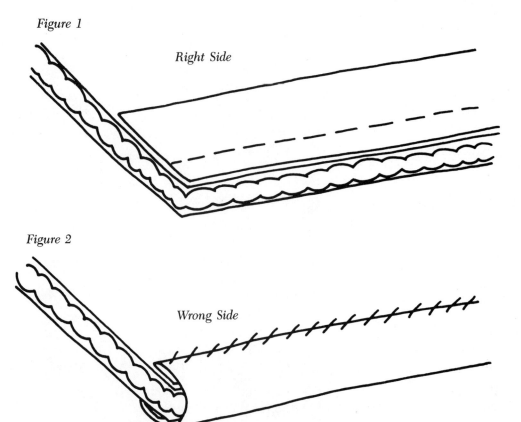

Right Side

Figure 2

Wrong Side

Gifts ══════════════════════ 6

Friends and relatives will admire your creativity and skill when they receive gifts you've made. Handmade gifts are unique and original, and people are apt to value them more than purchased gifts.

Every one of the home accessory designs in this book, from those in chapter 3 to the planters, pots, and wall decorations, make ideal housewarming and holiday gifts. Children's and infants' gifts could include small quilts, jewelry, bags, and purchased clothes decorated with crafts. Any of the fashion accessories make perfect presents for female friends and family members. For men, you could decorate a T-shirt or make various accessories, using some of the designs in this chapter. Office desk accessories, such as bargello-covered pencil containers and telephone book covers will please anyone whose office needs a warm, personal note.

This chapter features a method of covering books of any size with bargello, and using the same canvas-work technique for making a picture frame. Featured, too, is a needlepoint alphabet for making personalized gifts, and designs for greeting cards appropriate for all occasions—birthdays, anniversaries, holidays, and friendly greetings. Easy to make and inexpensive, these gifts are unusual and will delight their recipients.

Bargello Accessories

BOLDLY PATTERNED DESIGNS made with bargello can be fashioned into all sorts of useful, attractive accessories. The needlepoint canvas base gives them firmness and stability, making them ideal as protective and decorative coverings for books, photo albums, and telephone directories.

In this section there is an unusual bargello pattern for a paperback book cover. Using the book cover's construction technique, this pattern and other bargello patterns in this book can be expanded, working more pattern repeats lengthwise and widthwise, to make covers for larger books such as loose-leaf binders and photo albums. The patterns can also be adapted to create a collection of matching purse accessories, though the finishing techniques will be different for each item. One can include an eyeglass case, a change purse, a checkbook cover, and a charm for a key chain.

The bargello picture frame is another unique idea which can be imaginatively applied to other uses. This simple satin stitch pattern which forms neat, angular corners can be used to frame centers worked in more intricate bargello or needlepoint stitches. These make attractive squares for sewing onto pillows and purchased handbags. The bargello stitch pattern can be adjusted to the size of the picture to be framed, and can be made into a square or rectangular shape. This colorful, decorative frame would look great around a large portrait, a small snapshot, and all sorts of handmade needleworked and painted pieces.

Bargello Paperback Book Cover

(As shown in color plate 7)

THIS COVER FITS a standard $4\frac{1}{4}''$ x 7'' paperback book and is adjustable to the thickness of the book.

MATERIALS:

    9'' x 13'' piece of mono, duo, or interlock
       needlepoint canvas
    four colors, 1 ounce of each, in either 3-strand
       Persian-type yarn, or worsted yarn
    two $3\frac{1}{2}''$ x $7\frac{1}{2}''$ pieces of felt
    tapestry needle

Draw a line down the center of the canvas piece, then another line 1'' from the left edge, as shown in Figure 1. Begin working the pattern at Point X, covering the center line and two holes of canvas (Figure 2). Work Row 1 across until the stitched row fits loosely around the front cover, spine, and back cover of the book, with $\frac{1}{4}''$ extra lip extending beyond the edges of the book. Continue working the pattern row by row, arranging the colors as desired, and completing Row 10. Then turn the piece around and work Rows 2 through 10 on the other side of Row 1. (*Note:* One pattern repeat is featured in the chart. In working each row, once a segment is completed, simply return to the beginning of that segment of the pattern and repeat it, forming a continuous pattern across.)

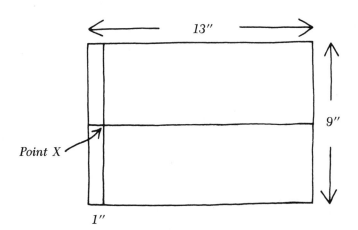

181

Figure 2

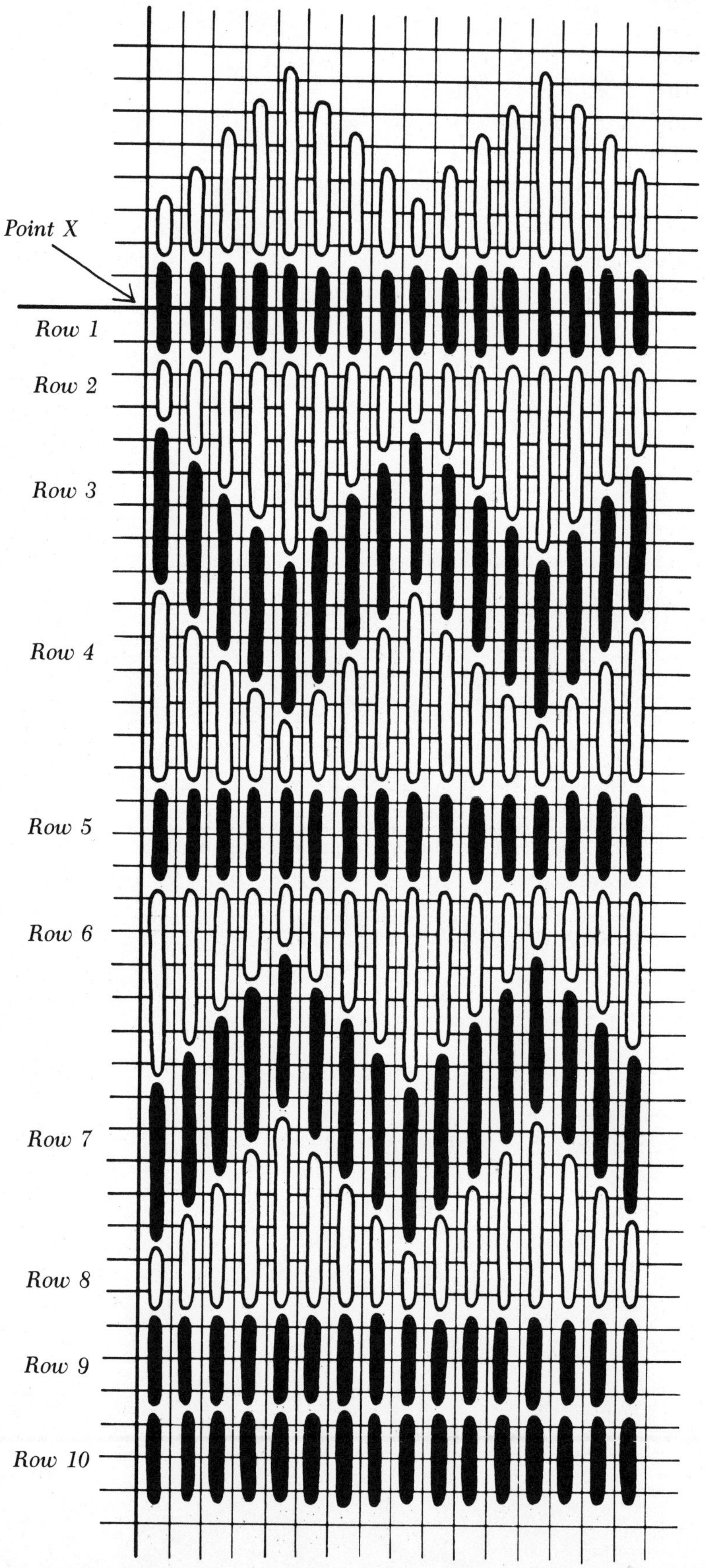

Point X

Row 1
Row 2
Row 3
Row 4
Row 5
Row 6
Row 7
Row 8
Row 9
Row 10

Block the stitched piece to the required size, if it has become distorted in stitching. Cut away the excess canvas, leaving a ½″ edge all around. Clip away the canvas at the four corners, ¼″ from the stitching. Fold back and sew down the edge all around, forming neat corners. On the wrong side pin a piece of felt to each side of the canvas, leaving a center strip uncovered which allows for the width of the book's spine. Trim the felt to fit if necessary. Hem the felt pieces securely to the edge of the canvas (Figure 3). If desired, blanket stitch or overcast stitch embroidery can be worked through all the layers at the very edge all around, using the same yarn used for stitching the pattern. This will form a more decorative edge.

Insert each cover of the book into one felt pocket (Figure 4). To make a cover for a book of any size using any of the bargello patterns shown in chapter 1, simply measure the book's length and the book's width, measuring around the book's front cover, spine and back cover. Add ½″ to the width measurement. Mark out the two dimensions on canvas and work the area in any bargello pattern. Complete it the same way as the paperback book cover, hemming down the raw edges and sewing felt pieces which are ¾″ narrower than the front cover to each of the two flaps.

Figure 3

Figure 4

Bargello Frame

(As shown in color plate 7)

MATERIALS:
- piece of 10-mesh needlepoint canvas to measure 8″ longer and wider than picture to be framed
- 3 or 4 colors, 1 ounce of each, of either 3-strand Persian-type yarn or worsted yarn
- 2 pieces of cardboard, each at least 6″ wider and longer than picture to be framed
- white glue or masking tape
- tapestry needle

Measure the dimensions of the picture to be framed. Mark these dimensions in the center of the canvas following the lines of the weave. At each of the four corners, draw a line extending diagonally out which cuts across the centers of a diagonal line of holes. These lines indicate where the pattern will form corners. Following Figure 1, stitch the first row around the original lines drawn, turning the corners as shown. Continue in rounds, stitching each round in a different color. Make the frame as wide as desired. Then work a round of chain stitch, working into every other hole, around the last and first rounds (as shown in the needlepoint section of chapter 1).

Block the stitched piece and measure the stitched area. Cut two pieces of cardboard to these dimensions. On one, cut out the center to measure the same as the unworked center of the canvas. Trim the excess canvas all around the stitched frame and cut out the unworked center, leaving a ½″ edge beyond the stitching. Clip the corners as shown in Figure 2. Place the bargello piece on top of the cardboard frame. Fold back and glue or tape the canvas edges to the back of the cardboard (Figure 3). Allow to dry.

Position and glue the photograph to the back of the bargello frame. Cover the other piece of cardboard with felt or adhesive-backed paper and glue it to the back of the picture and frame. Or simply glue a piece of felt to the back of the frame. If canvas shows along the outer edges of the finished frame, glue a thin strip of matching color felt around these edges to cover the canvas. To make a stand for the framed photograph, cut a piece of cardboard 4″ square. With a knife score the piece 1″ from one edge. Fold the piece along the scored line and glue the one-inch edge of the piece to the back of the frame, positioning it at a proper angle so the frame can stand.

Figure 1

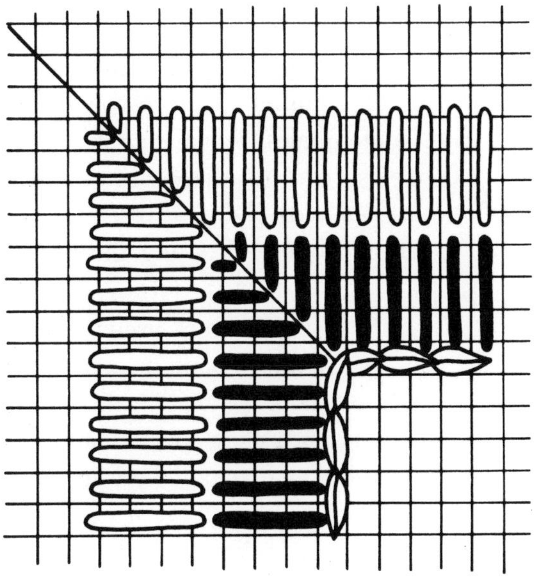

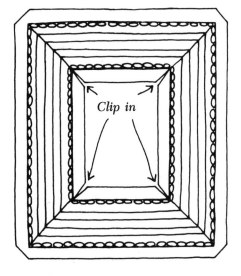

Figure 2

Clip in

Figure 3

Personalized Gifts

PERSONALIZED GIFTS CONTAINING inscriptions of names and initials are the ultimate "one-of-a-kind" creations. The graph of alphabet letters presented here is designed to be stitched on canvas using needlepoint techniques. It will help you create unusual, personalized presents for special people and special occasions.

A number of store-bought items, such as handbags, suitcases, change purses, eyeglass cases, and even tennis racket covers, can have personalized needlepointed appliqués sewn to them. The appliqués, stitched entirely in cross-stitch and with or without a decorative bargello border framing the lettered part, can contain either a full name or a set of initials.

The graph can be used for making clever door signs, designating a family's name to hang on a front door, or a child's name to hang on a bedroom door, or on a wall as a plaque. A colorful educational wall hanging for a child's room can be made by stitching all the letters on one piece of canvas, working each letter in a different color yarn.

Various bargello items described in this book, such as the checkbook cover, telephone book cover, or picture album, can have a stitched monogrammed section incorporated into the bargello pattern. A very unusual belt, handbag handle, or guitar strap can be created by stitching multiples of the wearer's name down its length.

Other possibilities for simple but ingenious personalized gifts include bookmarks, cans transformed into pencil holders by sewing stitched monogrammed canvas around them (see Bargello Planter, chapter 4), and greeting cards. For a more ambitious project, consider needlepointing a favorite poem or saying to use as a wall hanging.

Stitched on 10-holes-to-the-inch canvas the letters are $3/4''$ high, $1/2''$ wide. Done on 5-holes-to-the-inch canvas they are $1\frac{3}{8}''$ high, $7/8''$ wide. Based on these measurements, determine how large a piece of canvas you require for stitching the name or initials.

MATERIALS FOR SMALL LETTERS:
  Use 10-mesh canvas
  2 strands of 3-strand Persian-type yarn for the
    letters
  1 strand for stitching between and around the
    letters
  3 strands for a bargello border

MATERIALS FOR LARGE LETTERS:

    Use 5-mesh canvas

    1 strand of rug yarn or 2 strands of worsted
        yarn for the letters

    1 strand of worsted yarn for stitching between
        and around the letters

    2 strands of rug yarn for a bargello border

Following instructions for doing the cross stitch on canvas, shown in chapter 1, stitch all the letters first, leaving 2 meshes unworked between the letters and 3 meshes unworked between the rows for spacing. Then fill in around and between all the letters with finer cross stitches, using finer yarn.

If desired, work a bargello frame around the lettered area, following the stitch pattern given for the Bargello Frame. Stretch the completed piece around a mounting board and frame it. Or turn back and baste the raw canvas edges and use the piece as an appliqué.

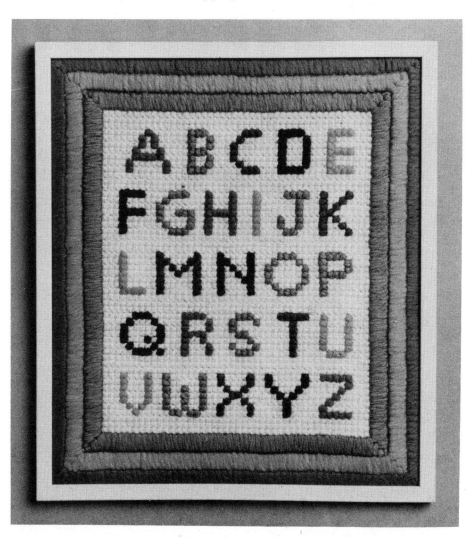

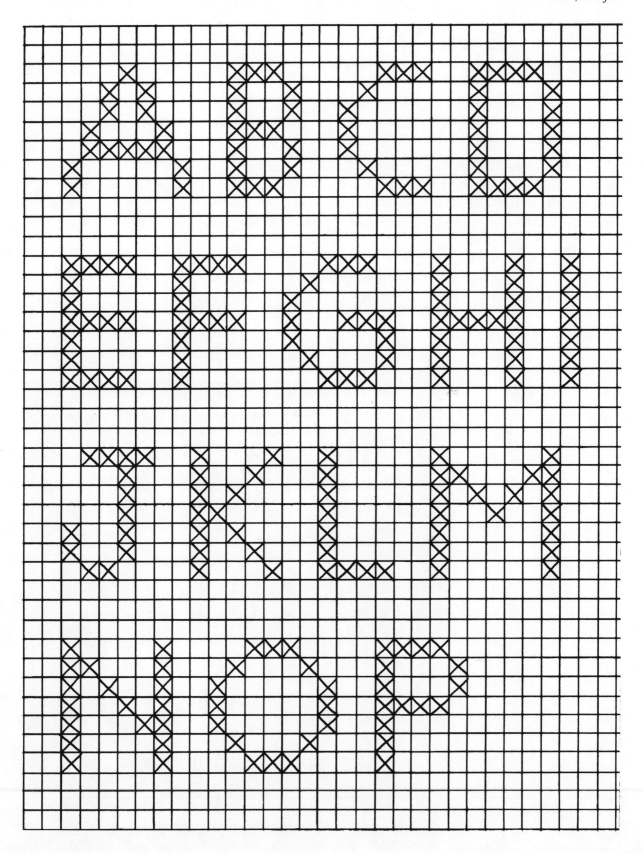

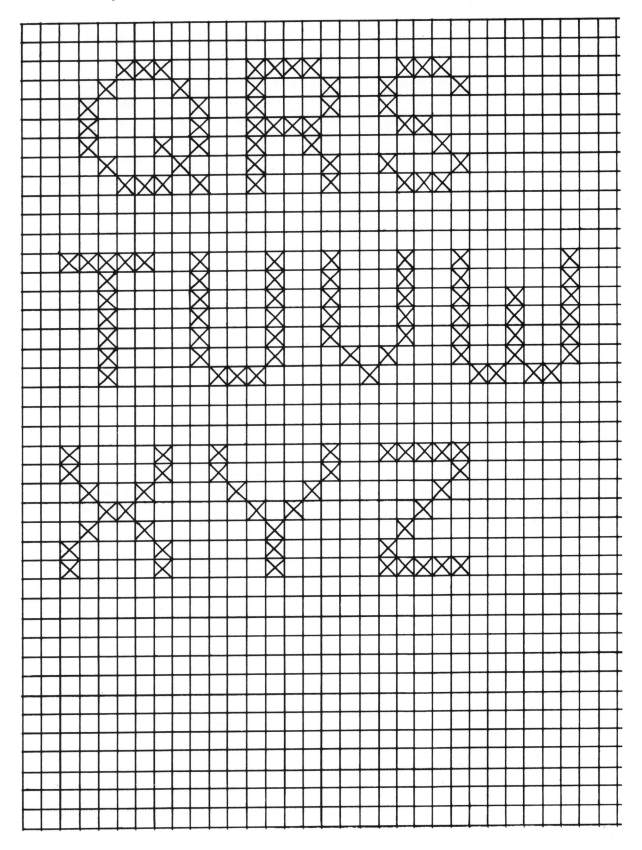

Greeting Cards

THOUGH THE SELECTION of imaginatively designed special-occasion cards appearing in stores is vast, an even more thoughtful and appreciated greeting would be a handmade one. Especially if you plan to give someone a gift you made yourself, accompanying it with a hand-crafted greeting card is a really clever and charming gesture.

The two embroidered greeting card designs presented here are appropriate for any occasion. Simply choose the saying that applies and the border of your choice, and trace both onto tracing paper, centering the saying inside the border. Following instructions in chapter 1, transfer the design to an 8″ x 8″ square of linen or cotton and stretch the fabric on an embroidery hoop. Then embroider the pattern in your choice of colors.

The floral border is made with easy to do basic embroidery stitches. The mirror-embroidered border involves an unusual technique of attaching round flat shapes to fabric by forming a stitched border around each one (see chapter 1). This method can easily be mastered with a little practice. Besides mirrors and flat, multicolored paillettes, coins can also form a very unusual border.

For making Christmas cards by the dozens, cut out the ½″ circles from stiff tinsel.

The completed embroidery can be framed in a standard 5″ x 7″ purchased frame. Or you can construct the frame yourself from cardboard, covering it with colorful vinyl adhesive paper. Whichever way this unique greeting card is presented, it will be appreciated and treasured.

BE MY
FRIEND

Mirror Border

(As shown in color plate 8)

MATERIALS:
> 8″ x 8″ piece of linen or cotton, embroidery
> needle and embroidery hoop
> scraps of embroidery floss in colors desired
> ½″ diameter round, flat circles such as mirrors
> or paillettes (large sequins)

Refer back to the instructions for embroidering with mirrors. Working throughout with 3 strands of embroidery floss and in colors desired, stitch the first border around each of the mirrors. With a contrasting color, work another border of evenly spaced lazy daisy stitches around each of the inner borders. Embroider the letters of the greeting with small backstitches.

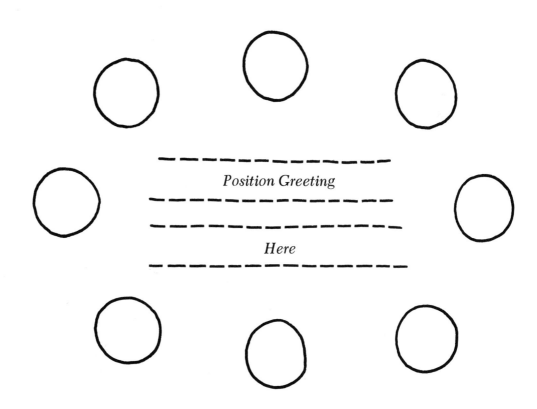

Floral Border

(As shown in color plate 8)

MATERIALS:

8″ x 8″ piece of linen or cotton, embroidery
needle and embroidery hoop
scraps of 3-strand crewel yarn or 6-strand
embroidery floss in colors specified

Note: Use 1 strand of crewel yarn or 3 strands of embroidery floss throughout. On the diagram, the letters refer to the color, the numbers indicate the stitch.

Colors

A—Green
B—Orange
C—Yellow
D—Red
E—Blue
F—Pink

Stitches

1—Split Stitch
2—Lazy Daisy Stitch
3—Straight Stitch
4—French Knot
5—Back Stitch
6—Satin Stitch

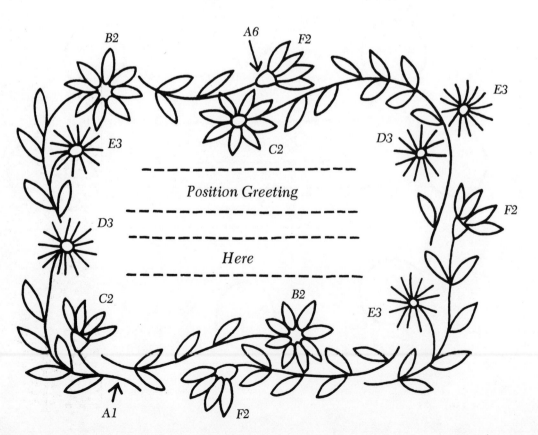

Working Procedure

1—Work all stems in green split stitch; all leaves are green lazy daisy stitch; bases of 3 pink and 1 yellow flowers are green satin stitch.

2—Following the diagram and the photograph in color plate 8 for color reference, work all the large flowers in lazy daisy stitch, all the small flowers in straight stitch.

3—Fill in centers of orange and yellow flowers with red French knots, the blue flowers with yellow French knots, the red flowers with orange French knots.

4—Embroider the letters of the greeting with small backstitches in any color desired.

HAPPY BIRTHDAY

HELLO

MERRY CHRISTMAS

SEASON'S GREETINGS

How to Make the Cardboard Frame

MATERIALS:
> two 8½″ x 7″ pieces of cardboard
> two 11″ x 9″ pieces of adhesive vinyl paper
> sharp cutting knife, such as an X-Acto or mat
> knife

Cut a 4½″ x 6″ opening in one of the cardboard pieces (Figure 1). Glue the adhesive paper to it. Cut away the center, leaving a ½″ edge for folding back the paper. Fold back the edges, gluing them to the inside of the frame (Figure 2). Cut away the excess fabric around the embroidery, leaving enough so it covers the frame's opening. Using scrap adhesive paper, tape the fabric to the inside of the frame (Figure 3). Place the other piece of cardboard on top of the back of the taped embroidery. Fold back and glue the outer edges of the adhesive paper, attaching the two pieces of cardboard together. Glue another piece of adhesive paper over the back of the frame, fully covering the cardboard.

Figure 1

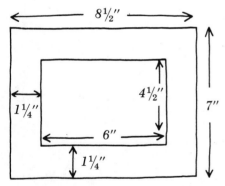

Figure 2

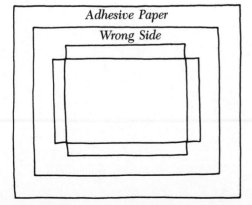

Figure 3

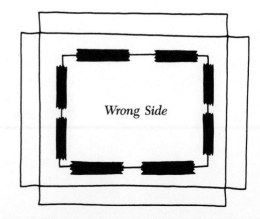

Where to Buy Craft Materials and Supplies

batting   Fabric stores

beads for macrame   Needlework sections of dime stores

belt buckle   Fabric stores, fabric departments of department stores

blank needlepoint canvas   Needlecraft supply stores

crochet cotton   Yarn stores; knitting materials sections of dime stores

cutting knives (X-ACTO, mat knives)   Hardware stores, art supply stores

embroidery hoop and embroidery floss   Needlecraft stores, needlecraft sections of dime stores

embroidery transfer pencils   Needlecraft stores; art supply stores

foam-filled board to use as macrame knotting board   Art supply stores

hole puncher (for crocheted appliquéd hanging)   Stationery stores

knitting yarn   Yarn stores; supermarkets; departments stores

masking tape   Hardware stores; art supply stores

mirrors, sequins, paillettes   Needlework sections of variety stores; needlecraft supply stores

persian-type yarn for needlepoint   Yarn and needlecraft supply stores

pillow stuffing   Fabric stores

plastic rings   Fabric stores; sewing notions departments of variety stores

raffia or synthetic straw   Yarn stores

ring (brass or other metal)   Hardware stores

ropes for macrame   Hardware stores; housewares departments of variety stores

tapestry needle   Yarn and needlecraft supply stores

trim for bargello-appliquéd pillow   Fabric stores

wood dowels   Hardware stores; lumber yards

wooden bag handles   Fabric stores; sewing notions departments of variety stores

Metric Equivalency Chart

CONVERTING INCHES TO CENTIMETERS

This chart gives the standard equivalents
as approved by the Pattern Fashion Industry.

mm—millimeters   cm—centimeters

CHANGING INCHES TO MILLIMETERS AND CENTIMETERS
(Slightly rounded for your convenience.)

inches	mm	cm	inches	cm	inches	cm
$\frac{1}{8}$	3mm		7	18	29	73.5
$\frac{1}{4}$	6mm		8	20.5	30	76
$\frac{3}{8}$	10mm or	1 cm	9	23	31	79
$\frac{1}{2}$	13mm or	1.3cm	10	25.5	32	81.5
$\frac{5}{8}$	15mm or	1.5cm	11	28	33	84
$\frac{3}{4}$	20mm or	2cm	12	30.5	34	86.5
$\frac{7}{8}$	22mm or	2.2cm	13	33	35	89
1	25mm or	2.5cm	14	35.5	36	91.5
$1\frac{1}{4}$	32mm or	3.2cm	15	38	37	94
$1\frac{1}{2}$	38mm or	3.8cm	16	40.5	38	96.5
$1\frac{3}{4}$	45mm or	4.5cm	17	43	39	99
2	50mm or	5cm	18	46	40	101.5
$2\frac{1}{2}$	65mm or	6.5cm	19	48.5	41	104
3	75mm or	7.5cm	20	51	42	106.5
$3\frac{1}{2}$	90mm or	9cm	21	53.5	43	109
4	100mm or	10cm	22	56	44	112
$4\frac{1}{2}$	115mm or	11.5cm	23	58.5	45	114.5
5	125mm or	12.5cm	24	61	46	117
$5\frac{1}{2}$	140mm or	14cm	25	63.5	47	119.5
6	150mm or	15cm	26	66	48	122
			27	68.5	49	124.5
			28	71	50	127

Index